MIRRORED REALITIES

MIЯRORED REALITIES

A Collection of Prose & Poetry

LUW Press

Salt Lake City, Utah

MIRRORED REALITIES
A Collection of Prose & Poetry
Copyright © 2016 LUW Press

ISBN-13: 978-0-9882367-3-8 (LUW Press)
ISBN-10: 0-9882367-3-7

Book format and cover design by Mark E. Moody.

For now we see through a glass, darkly...

—1 Corinthians 13:12

SPECIMENS

ALL TWISTED UP

J. Anthony Gohier

It seemed he tied her tongue in knots
by giving her a smile,
and she pickled Peter's peppers
like it was going out of style.

But sweetly whispered nothings really
offered them no clue
of the Tweedle-Beetle Puddle-Paddle
Battle to ensue

How did that little busy bee
improve his golden days,
while wrapping evening memories
in murky twilight haze?

The fault was not completely hers;
I'll never say it was,
despite the way she drew him in
with gently smiling jaws.

There had been times he asked as their
toy boat set out to space
if that peck of pickled peppers may
have somehow been misplaced.

Yet still the ragged rascal ran
around those rugged rocks,
and all the pretty ponies kept
their secrets like Fort Knox.

It ended with a simple thing,
he barely thought would matter,
but that bit of bitter butter
really bittered Betty's batter.

Her burning ears were hanging low.
The diamond ring turned brass.
The cat's back in the cradle,
in the house now made of glass.

The lion to his unicorn,
she stopped him where he stood,
and let's just say, that woodchuck had
chucked all the wood he could.

At last, the toes of Moses turned out
not to smell like roses,
regardless of whatever either
party still supposes.

Now he's off to unique New York
to be a man of means,
and she's still selling seashells by
the seashores of her dreams.

Their rhyming game was at an end;
a blink and both had missed it—
how a thing that seemed so simple could
have ended up so twisted.

SCREEN TIME

E. B. Wheeler

I have a parenting problem. My four-year-old is bored with *My Little Ponies: Friendship is Magic*, but I'm not ready to give it up. Usually I sing "Halleluiah" when she's ready to move on from a favorite show. I couldn't say *adios* to *Dora the Explorer* fast enough. Sure, it teaches a little Spanish, but when is Zoey ever going to need to tell anyone that she's a map? And that "*Soy el mapa, soy el mapa*" song would go round and round in my head all day after she watched it.

What's worse, though, was the stare. If you've seen Dora, you know what I'm talking about.

Dora asks, "Do *you* want to go to the circus?"

Then she violates the sacred fourth wall and stares at you with those big, unblinking brown eyes until you squirm.

Usually Zoey shouts "Yes!" with all the enthusiasm of a kid who hasn't figured out that Dora can't hear her.

No matter how Zoey answers, Dora just says, "I love the circus!"

There are people like that in my neighborhood. I see them when we're out walking, and they say, "Hi! How're you?"

I usually say, "Fine, how 'bout you?" But I could also say, "I'm terrible. This morning the baby smeared poo all over the cat, and while I was giving them both a bath, Zoey decided to make a cake by pouring flour and eggs into the blender and turning it on. We're not taking a walk right now. We're running away from home. But, how're you?"

Either way, they'd smile and say, "Oh, I'm good. See you around."

Yeah, I get enough vacant stares in real life; I don't need them from the television too.

Then there's *Curious George*. I didn't understand the appeal of that show until I had a preschooler, but now I see the genius behind it. Four-year-olds can relate to George, maybe a little too well. He had Zoey running around the house making monkey noises and narrating her actions in third person.

"Zoey saw that Mommy was making cookies. Zoey wanted to taste the dough, so she slid a chair into the kitchen. Oops! Zoey knocked flour and eggs all over the floor. Zoey hid in the cupboard while Mommy cleaned up the mess."

Mommy is not amused.

I do miss *Shaun the Sheep*, but banning him from the house was the only way to undo all the bad manners he was teaching Zoey. She still produces some rather impressive belches during dinner to remind us of that particular TV phase.

Those shows have nothing on *My Little Ponies*, though. The musical numbers are catchy, the dialogue is surprisingly clever, and the message of each episode is the kind of sticky sweet you don't mind chewing on, like taffy.

Like most kids' shows, it's all just a spectacular marketing ploy. Each of the six main ponies has a distinct trait—generosity, loyalty, honesty, kindness, laughter, and magic—that combine to create the unconquerable power of friendship. If you give in and get just one pony, how can you not buy the other five? They need each other! And these two-inch tall pieces of plastic start at twelve bucks each, so if your child discovers they can actually own their favorite pony friends, you'd better be good at catching clearance sales or surviving the Black Friday stampedes.

Even while recognizing Hasbro's evil genius, I've let the show draw me in. I can lip sync with all the songs. I watch for cameo appearances by fan favorites like Dr. Whooves and Derpy Hooves.

I've gone out of my way to read the discussions by physicists about how fast Pegasus Rainbow Dash would actually have to fly to create a sonic rain-boom (Yes, this scientific discussion actually exists, and a little over 4,000 mph is the lowest calculation I've seen).

How can I stop watching it now, especially with season four coming up? I need to know what's going to happen now that (spoiler alert!) Twilight Sparkle is a princess and Rainbow Dash joined the Wonderbolts. Sure, I could steal a few precious moments from my scanty free time to sit alone in the dark and watch it, but it wouldn't be the same.

Part of the magic was finding something that my daughter and I could enjoy together. Yes, I like reading books to her, or taking her for walks, or even letting her torture my hair in her beauty shop, but I'm always in "Mom mode" when we do those things: teaching, guiding, watching. There are so few times when she and I are just two people sharing a moment of pure delight. Finding a ladybug in the garden, watching the birds hop and flutter around the feeder, laughing when the baby tries to put a diaper on the cat: these are all precious, but also spontaneous. I can't control them like I can the computer screen that brings us our special TV show.

Of course, I can't control my daughter either, as she grows into her own person. Like when I offer to help her practice gymnastics.

"No, I can do it myself, Mommy. Watch!" She shows off lop-sided cartwheels. If she would let me, I could help her keep her legs straight. But I remain a spectator, smiling past my heartache as she figures out how to do it herself.

I relish each chance to create bonds with her, to keep her from wandering too far someday, even if that means learning the words to the "Winter Wrap Up" song and discovering that down-to-earth Applejack is my favorite pony. Because I also learned that Zoey's favorite is Rainbow Dash: brave, loyal, headstrong, and always looking for the next challenge. So as my daughter races across the yard, arms spread like wings and hair streaming out behind her, I understand her that much better.

EMBERS

Marie Tollstrup

Embers still warm me despite
his flame dying two years ago.
Farewell to days in the sun.
Farewell to nights in his arms.

Love-waves rose as a rolling tide
for thirty-seven years.
Now his extinguished blaze
retains an ember's glow.

We adventured to foreign cities,
flew down mountain peaks.
Tennis balls obeyed our commands,
golf balls found their mark.
Side by side we contrived dinners,
nurtured more by love than food.

While reading books,
his baritone voice soothed,
calmed my agitated days.
We held hands in bed,
fused while sleeping.

Embers light flickering scenarios,
confirming the gift I had lived.
Farewell to days in the sun.
Farewell to nights in his arms.

SCIAMACHY

Tim Tarbet

Ben lay curled into a ball. His back ached. The sunlight streamed through the window. He covered his face with a blanket and rolled over. He closed his eyes, but sleep would not come. He sat up and swung his feet over the edge of the bed. Finally getting up? Took you long enough, he thought. His stomach grumbled at him. Functionally, he was hungry. It had been... How long since he'd eaten last? Two days? Three? A while.

He stood up, grabbed his phone, and shuffled to the kitchen. Pot. Water. Instant noodles. He turned the dial on the stove to high and pulled out his phone. With a few dull taps on the screen he opened a social app and scrolled, not reading the words. He refreshed the page and scrolled again. He closed it, then opened it again. Addict. You're rotting your brain. His arm fell to his side and he clicked off the phone. He tossed it on the counter. The water bubbled and steamed.

Plastic crinkled as the noodles slid into the boiling water. Broken fragments tumbled onto the stovetop. Slob. Can't even make instant noodles without making a mess, can you? The microwave chirped when he jammed his finger against the timer button. Two minutes.

Ben grabbed a chair, rested his elbows on the table, and buried his face in his hands. Breathe in. Breathe out. In. Out. Hold.

The world stopped, did not exist. There was only darkness, hot and close on his mind, like a sweltering summer night. Nothing was, nor would be again, so long as Ben held his breath. The dark surrounded him like a blanket wrapped too tight, quiet and stifling. His lungs burned, throat swallowed.

Finally Ben's hands hit the table top with a slap and he sucked in air. He hadn't left the apartment in days. He clenched his jaw and ran his fingers through his hair. Of course, it wasn't like he was really going to do anything, anyway. His accomplishments for the week amounted to Skyrim. Fifty hours of Skyrim. His stomach churned and he clenched his hands in his hair.

That's the only thing you're really good at, isn't it? Video games.

Fast food? Temporary position only. Landscaping? Too weak. Clerical work? Not qualified. He'd be lucky if he could find himself another job, much less one that he enjoyed.

He leaned back in his chair, stared at the ceiling. He glanced at the job applications that cluttered the table. They were from local restaurants and department stores. Other people were nurses or teachers or scientists.

Or boxers.

The timer beeped. He got to his feet and shuffled to the stove.

Not even that good at video games, he thought. Better than average, maybe, but nowhere near major league. The cabinet door creaked when he swung it open and pulled out the colander. It clattered when he dropped it in the sink. He'd never have the twitch reflexes that the big league FPS players had, or the swift, tactical cunning of the RTS and MOBA players had.

The noodles writhed like eels in the boiling water, then fell to the bottom when he pulled the pot off the stove. He poured the broth, noodles and all, into the colander, then dumped the noodles back into the pot. The flavor packet rustled as he opened it and dumped the vomit yellow powder into the pot with the noodles. He grabbed a fork and stirred the mass as he made his way back to the table. The noodles looked like so many lifeless yellow worms by the time he sat down. He stared at them, watched the steam disappear, then twirled his fork, making a little spool of slimy yarn.

The spool made it about halfway to his mouth, then froze midair. It hung there like a mass of caterpillars caught in spider silk, almost writhing as it hung from the fork. As he stared at it his stomach churned and bile rose to the back of his throat. The fork clattered back into the pot.

He dumped the noodles into the trash with yesterday's attempt at a meal, and that of the day before that. You're wasting food again. The pot and fork went into the sink with the other dishes. Going to run out of pots, soon.

He made his way back to the bedroom, closed the door, and collapsed on his chair.

Waste of skin.

Ben took a deep breath, held it, let it out slowly. That's all he was, wasn't he? He wasn't smart. He wasn't tough. He wasn't outgoing. He was the guy people kept around as a pity project. He rubbed his eyes, ground his palms into his eye sockets. Colors blossomed under his eyelids.

Useless.

He looked at the desk drawer, contemplated its contents. He probably should, shouldn't he? He deserved it. He didn't matter. Nobody cared.

The ones who did care were wrong.

One hand closed around the drawer handle and slid it open, and the other rummaged around inside until he found what he was looking for. He pinched the razor blade between his fingers and held it up to his face.

It was a normal razor: gray, rectangular, identical to the million others that were stamped out, dulled, and thrown away every year. There was a box of fifty more in the kitchen cabinet, but this one was his. He'd hidden it away months ago, convenient and innocuous in his desk drawer.

He'd used it before.

He clamped his jaw and watched the little blade, turned it over and over in his fingers. The edge glinted in the dim light, inviting.

He brought it to his neck, pressed the razors edge against his skin. A vein struggled against the steel. He pressed a little harder, dug in a little deeper. Pain bloomed at the corners of the tiny blade. Ben took a breath and flicked his wrist. Skin parted and blood dripped.

It felt good.

He only wished he had the will to push just a little bit harder. Finish it. Get it over with.

Ben's neck burned as he looked down, resting his elbows on his knees. Slowly, he leaned forward and brought the razor to his arm.

He was better at these. Not such a pansy. He dug an edge into the crook of his elbow and dragged it to his wrist, skin sliding open and blood beading along the shallow cut. It was strangely grounding, making the lacerations, watching the blood bead on his skin. The tension leeched out of his shoulders, his mind went quiet. He could forget everything else, let it all go and just focus on the slow burning lines he drew in his flesh and the pain.

Ben moved up to the shoulder and cut one, two, three times. He couldn't say why he cut where he did. It just felt right. Down the elbow, following the bone. Across the bicep. Back of the wrist. Knuckles.

Blood dripped down his arm, hot on his skin. The cuts burned, ached. He wondered how much blood it would take before he felt cold. He'd never gone that far before.

He just might this time, though.

He brought the razor to the inside of his wrist, next to the first cut he'd made, and slowly dragged it to the crook of his elbow, pushing deeper, harder than he normally did. Skin parted, then muscle and veins. His hand shook, instinct that told him to jerk his arm away barely held in check.

It felt good.

Ben clenched his teeth, pushed harder, and the pain became deeper. His hands shook, nerves screamed. He pushed on. He was going to finish this cut. He didn't care about the pain, didn't care about the damage. He might not be able to do anything else right, but this he could do.

Halfway there. Blood dripped from his wrist onto the carpet; he'd have to clean that up later. Pain beat at him, railed on his nerves, turned his stomach. He clenched his teeth. Just a little farther...

The bedroom door slammed open. "Guess who's back, lover boy, and ready for some..."

Ben's stomach clenched. Ruth stood frozen in the doorway, halfway through taking off her shirt. Jacket, luggage, boxing gloves, hat made a trail to the front door. His hat. She'd taken it with her for good luck. Her mouth hung open as she stared at him. She had a split lip and a black eye.

"Ben?"

Ben's cheeks burned, his mouth suddenly dry. Blood dripped from his wrist.

"Ben, what are you doing?" Her voice was small, barely above a whisper, and shook around the edges.

Ben tore his eyes away from hers, focusing on their bed, hiding the razor behind his back. He shifted in his chair, uncomfortably aware that he was wearing nothing but his socks and his boxers.

"You weren't supposed to be back until tomorrow."

"What the fuck does that have to do with anything?" she shouted. Her shirt hit the floor with a quiet whump.

"I... I didn't want you to see this," Ben whispered. The words stuck in his throat. He wanted to say more. Tell her that he was sorry. Explain why. Tell her that it wasn't a big deal, he wouldn't have gone all the way.

Tell her that even if he had, she would be better off without him.

Instead, he just sat there.

Ruth moved closer to him. "Ben, give me the razor blade." Her voice was surprisingly steady.

Ben felt his fingers tighten around the slim piece of metal.

"Ben, I need you to give me that razor blade." Ben opened his eyes and saw Ruth kneeling in front of him. He looked away, shifted the arm behind his back.

Ruth reached around him, pressing their bodies together. He felt her fingers wrap around the blade.

"Give. Me. The. Fucking. Razor." She punctuated each word with a tug, the metal finally sliding free of Ben's fingers. She tossed it into the trash can where it landed with a clack. Slowly, Ben slipped his arm from behind his back and grabbed his shoulder. The skin was slick under his fingers, and the cuts burned from the sudden pressure.

All at once, Ruth wrapped her arms around him and buried her face in his neck. Her shoulders shook as she squeezed him painfully. She ran her fingers though his hair again and again as she quietly cried against him. Ben sat motionless. Her tears dripped down his chest. Then, he slid his good arm around his lover and held her tight. Wetness burned the corners of his eyes but refused to fall.

The two held each other, gently rocking. Then Ruth pulled away and grabbed Ben by the shoulders.

"Hey. Look at me."

Ben glanced up and only met her eyes for a second before turning away.

She grabbed his face and pulled it close to her own. Tears stained her face. "Look at me."

His eyes flicked up to meet hers again, before falling, focusing on her nose. She tried to follow, dropping her head, looking up at him. "We're gonna get through this, ok? Ok?"

Ben nodded.

"You know I love you, right?"

"You shouldn't. You could do better than a loser like me."

Ben hadn't meant to say those words. He'd thought them over and over again since the day he and Ruth had gotten together, but he hadn't meant to say them.

Ben's head snapped sideways. His cheek stung and his vision spun. Before he'd had a chance to recover, Ruth grabbed his head again and pressed their foreheads together.

"Don't you say that, don't you fucking say that ever again. Don't you even think that. I love you too much to let you throw it away like that. I. Love. You. You got that?"

Ben nodded quickly, raising a hand to his cheek.

"Good. Now don't you forget it." She shook him as she spoke.

Ben rubbed his cheek and nodded. Pain simmered where Ruth hit him. She grabbed his arm, held it up. He could feel her shake. She sniffed.

"This one..." Ruth choked. "This is going to need stitches."

She grabbed her shirt off the floor and moved to press it against the wound. Ben tried to jerk away, but Ruth held him fast.

"Stop being an ass. Hold still."

"Your shirt—"

"I'd rather lose a shirt than a boyfriend, now hold still."

The cuts stung, burned, and the shirt turned red as the blood advanced through the fabric.

"Hold this there. Hold it. Good. Keep pressure on it." She lifted his chin and covered her mouth with her other hand. Tears gathered at the corners of her eyes, and she ran a finger along the half crusted blood on his neck. She drew a shuddering breath and swallowed.

"Come on. We're going to the hospital."

A PROMISE OF TOMORROW

Sandy Roberts

My son doesn't understand.
"Why do you do it?" he asks.
"You are sick, you need to stop.
It hurts your back, your knees."
My son doesn't understand
The joy that fills my soul
With the first crocus bloom,
Or the satisfaction of tiredness.
My son doesn't understand
That fruit tastes better
Picked fresh from the tree,
Juice running down my chin.
My son doesn't understand
The satisfaction in a refuse pile
Built by my own hand and sweat,
A labor of love to my garden.
My son doesn't understand
That even in the sleep of winter
My garden holds promise,
A hope that I will see spring.
My son doesn't understand
The joy of a growing bouquet
A riot of color bursting forth
Adding beauty to my world.

My son doesn't understand
The connection when I kneel
Where my grandmother knelt
To tend the flowers she loved.
My son doesn't understand
That even in pain and loneliness
The earth brings peace to my soul
And an assurance of tomorrow.
My son doesn't understand Me.

SELENE'S REPLACEMENT

D A Gordon

Of all the Grecian woes,
Oh goddess sing.
—Iliad

{ 1 } EARLY IN THE FIRST CENTURY, AD

N othing ever changed here. Within and without, the palace
and grounds—even the Moon itself—appeared as they
always had.

Selene rose, straightened the folds of her lavender gown, and
walked to the large window separating her throne room from the
courtyard. Beyond the bleak horizon hovered the blue and white
planet, presenting a shock of color against the inky backdrop of
space. From her lunar palace Earth looked the same as it always
had, but she knew all too well that life on the planet had changed
a great deal in the last two thousand years.

She twirled a strand of wavy hair. As a Titan goddess she could
wield godly powers against both man and the elements by causing
visions and hallucinations, governing light, and even cloaking her

presence. She could ride through the cloud-shrouded gate to dine on mushrooms with the Olympians or land on Earth to visit mankind. She didn't have many options, but the ones she had were unique.

Nevertheless she struggled against a burgeoning desire for change.

Wrapping her arms around her chest she turned from the courtyard to pace down a wide hall, made wider still by its emptiness. Despite her fear of Zeus and her innate sense of duty, she found herself thinking the unthinkable: gaining her freedom. Although she wasn't clear on what she would do with freedom if she had it, the thought of being released from this tiresome duty haunted her. Most days she shrugged it off. For someone like her, a Titan who survived Zeus' overthrow of the ancient rulers, freedom was not an option.

Or was it?

She knew just the being to ask.

The Moon goddess found herself in the dining hall. "Zella," she called, "are you here?"

Her handmaiden rushed into view. "Yes, my lady."

"Please tell the stable manager I want to leave for Earth this morning."

"Yes ma'am. Would you like me to pack for you?"

Selene smiled. After all these years Zella remained the same, pleasant and eager to help; Selene loved her like a sister. "No thank you, Zella. This should be a short trip. But could you bring me a glass of nectar before I leave?"

"Yes, I'll bring it right away."

∽

Looking for Pan, Selene drove her chariot through the celestial tunnel to Greece and then to the island of Skyros. Ever since the Roman invasion of Greece, Pan lived in a secluded cabin on this island. Normally Selene would not make a special trip to visit him, for he had a well-earned reputation for seducing humans and gods alike. But besides being the god of shepherds and flocks, he possessed a wealth of knowledge about the Titans, including their powers and limitations. She planned to tap that expertise.

She wouldn't trust the goat-god alone in a room, but she knew she could trust his discretion regarding her inquiry, for Pan owed no allegiance to Zeus. With her chariot cloaked she flew above the trees until she spotted a wooden cabin with a thatched roof, just the type of home Pan would build. She parked near a copse of beech trees and released her horses to graze. Before she reached the cabin, Pan rushed to greet her.

"What's this?" he said. "A vision of beauty has landed in my woods."

Selene dipped her chin. The two exchanged a few pleasantries, and Selene firmly removed his hand from her hip. Pan nodded.

"Well then," he said, "what brings the delectable Moon goddess to my island?"

"I have a pressing question, and I thought you could help."

"In that case, I hope to be of service." He led her to a stone covered patio surrounded by flowering trees and shrubs. The nearby fountain was alive with birds and frogs. The sounds and smells of the garden mixed with the salty air delighted her senses. She wondered what it must be like to dwell every day in a colorful place like this, so vibrant and alive.

Pan invited her to sit on a bench, while he perched on a nearby stool. Selene crossed her legs and nervously smoothed her gown. Looking at her hands, she started.

"As you know," she began, "I have been the Moon goddess for thousands of years."

"Yes, you have." Pan plucked a tall stalk of wild grass and stuck it in his mouth.

"For as long as I can remember," she continued, "I've had to restrict the time I could spend on Earth."

"That's true. Your time away from the Moon is limited."

"One-fourth of a cycle isn't long," Selene continued. "Sometimes I want to stay longer."

Pan stroked his thin beard. "Well, this planet is certainly greener than the Moon, and there is much more to do."

Selene re-crossed her legs and gave Pan a serious look. "But I'm curious. What is the *worst* that can happen to me if I resist the pull of my throne and don't return on the seventh day?"

Pan swallowed and raised an eyebrow. "So *that's* what you have in mind. Interesting." He reached for another stalk of grass. "From what I know if you actually do succeed in resisting your throne's pull and fail to return to your palace, your body will start to wither."

Selene frowned. "Wither?"

"Maybe 'waste away' would be more accurate, but either way, if you don't honor the call to return to your palace, the smooth skin on your lovely body will start to shed. The longer you remain on Earth beyond your deadline, the more your body will slough away until all that remains of your beautiful self is a pile of celestial dust."

"Dust."

"Yes, much like the powder that surrounds your palace."

"Oh." Selene shifted in her seat, uneasy with the image he'd created.

"It appears that godly beings love drama," he continued. "Remember the Hebrew story of Lot's wife?"

"Hmm, yes."

"Your transformation would be slower but similar, like *dust to dust*."

Selene turned away to peer through the olive trees. The afternoon sun played across the surface of the Aegean Sea, making the water shimmer like a silver tray. For a moment she entertained thoughts of finding a place of her own on these islands, then she remembered the pile of dust and stopped.

Pan leaned forward. "Alas, Selene. Just as trees need light and goats need food, the Moon needs a godly presence on its throne. This time restriction continues to rule over you, my lady, whether you would have it or not."

She silenced a groan.

"Unfortunately this is your Fate. Along with your impressive powers of persuasion and illusion, you have this responsibility."

"You mean this *burden*."

"Well, that too." For a moment the two sat in silence, Pan looking at Selene as she looked at the ground. At last Pan slipped off his stool, saying, "Excuse me for a moment. I'll be right back." He entered the small cabin and returned with a canvas bag, which he placed on Selene's lap.

"You should take these with you. Who knows when we'll meet again."

Selene peered into the heavy bag. "Rocks?"

Pan smiled. "Not ordinary rocks. Each crusty exterior contains a moonstone crystal. When the crystals are polished and connected they can yield great power, especially for someone like you."

Pan returned to his stool. "Selene, trust me on this. Someday you will understand their power, and that's when the Magick will work for you."

Selene set it on the bench and said, "Thank you." Despite his cryptic explanation, she would not press him. Over the centuries Pan had given her impressive gifts, like her silver chariot, the immortal white horses, and her scepter, so he must have a good reason for handing her this bag and its curious contents. Pan explained the importance of weaving the polished crystals into a strand or braid to increase their power, then he dropped the subject and made a curious request.

"Would you indulge me in a bit of retrospection? I would enjoy reminiscing about the way things used to be." He wanted to speak of happier, grander times, back when the Zeus held glorious parties, when the gods played marvelous games and the music shook the halls of Mount Olympus, back when everyone laughed as hard as they fought. Selene readily agreed. For a while the two sounded like classmates as they recalled the happy times they spent with their fellow gods and immortals. Although Pan often laughed as they talked, Selene noticed an unusual sadness about him, something deep and troubling, but she thought it impolite to pry.

When the coral streaks of sunset stretched across the sky, Selene stood. She thanked Pan for his poignant advice, the pleasant conversation, and the curious bag of stones. He watched as she harnessed the horses. When she climbed aboard and took the reins, Pan bowed.

"Until next time, my lady."

She nodded. "Yes, until next time."

During her ride home she struggled to staunch her thoughts of living a different kind of life. She must be content with life as it is, regardless of restrictions or shortcomings.

A year later rumors of Pan's demise spread throughout the islands, then north to Arcadia and Macedonia, and at last to Selene's palace.

She heard conflicting accounts of his disappearance; some said he passed away while others claimed he went into seclusion. She didn't know which stories to believe, but she never saw him or heard from him again.

❦

Back on the Moon, Selene and her servants took turns chiseling and scraping the rocks, then polishing the crystals. Months later the twelve crystals were as smooth as her marble statues. The feldspar gems varied in size but most resembled a hen's egg. As Pan suggested, Selene used a dozen plaited fibers to connect the stones by weaving them into a large braid, keeping them an equal distance apart. Unsure what to do with the enchanting but heavy creation, she wrapped it in a piece of velvet and placed it in a niche beside the statue of Hecate, asking the goddess of Magick to watch over it.

Then she forgot about the braided crystals for over a thousand years.

{ 2 } SPRING 1783

"By the gods," Selene muttered, clenching her fist. She had vowed never to drum her fingers, no matter how many hours she sat here. Zeus used to drum his fingers before roaring judgment against someone who displeased him, and she still feared his wrath. In all this time since the Thunder King took over Olympus, Selene had done nothing that might upset him.

Until now.

She toyed with her pendant. If Zeus knew what she planned he would be furious. She could imagine his thunderous voice shaking the columns of his palace, but she would not allow fear to stop her. She had heard nothing from the Olympians for centuries. Perhaps that door of communication had closed; if so, it was a blessing. By the time Zeus discovered her duplicity, she would be as hard to find as a single memory in a cloud of dreams.

Her plan was a good one, and it would work... *it had to.*

"Excuse me, my lady." The words pulled her back to the moment.

"Do you need anything else?" Zella asked.

"No thank you. You can take my cup."

Zella took the cup and nodded. "Good evening."

Selene smiled. "See you tomorrow."

Selene faced the courtyard. At one end she saw the edge of the stable and at the other end loomed the opening to her pathway to Earth. That celestial portal afforded her a semblance of freedom. For ages that had been enough, but not anymore.

⌘

In the morning a golden hippogriff flew out of the portal and landed near the stables. The creature's squawk sounded like an enormous peacock, rattling windows and frightening the animals. The stable attendants shrank from the unusual beast, but stood their ground when the god who brought fire to mankind leapt from the animal's back and removed his helmet. Prometheus approached the stable workers.

"Have no fear," he said as he handed one of them the reins. "This creature belongs to a friend who assured me the animal will behave if fed regularly." Prometheus handed another attendant a hefty bag of meat and bones. "If he gives you any trouble, let me know." They nodded.

He handed another bag to the third attendant. "The fruit and fish in this bag are for all of you."

They thanked him and led the large animal to the stable. Prometheus turned toward Earth, so far away and yet so near. Through the swirling clouds he saw the large ocean. Although he hadn't seen Zeus in ages, he dared not visit the Moon while Greece was in full view of Selene's palace. After Heracles freed him from Zeus' torment, Prometheus stayed far away from Greece, traveling north to live among the Scandinavians and their remaining gods. For centuries he evaded the Titans and Olympians until he quite accidentally ran into Selene. That encounter transformed his life. Now here he was, leaving his realm of safety, traveling to the Moon, and tempting Fate.

But Selene was worth the risk. With her he had a chance to replace the life Zeus stole from him.

Prometheus turned away from the blue planet to see Selene standing on the palace steps. His heart leapt. Her pale skin, long hair, silver dress and lavender cloak offered a welcome contrast to the bleak lunar surface. She wasn't just beautiful, she was captivating. He rushed across the courtyard and bounded up the steps where he grabbed the regal goddess and lifted her in the air.

"There you are," he said, swinging her around. As he held her, she buried her fingers in his hair and pressed her lips against his neck. Yes, this was what he wanted. He carried her through the large doors, across the Sumerian rugs, down the hall lined with statues, and into her private quarters.

"I'm so glad you could come," she said. "I dared not hope too much."

He squeezed her until she gasped, then set her down and kissed her face, her neck, her hair. "I have missed you," he whispered.

"And you have been missed."

Prometheus shed his fur coat and helped her with her cloak. He wanted to kiss her over and over, without stopping, but instead he held her at arm's length. He needed to know if their plan was still on schedule.

"Tell me more about this young woman you found," he said. "Is she still a good choice?"

"Oh, yes. She is perfect, in many ways. She has a unique combination of beauty, poise, cunning, and audacity."

He cupped Selene's chin and lowered his voice. "She sounds like someone I know." When she smiled, he marveled at how the fireplace light danced in her eyes.

"This young lady is strong willed," Selene continued. "She plans to defy her father's wishes by fleeing to another country, but that would place her in mortal danger. The roads in Europe are not safe for a young woman traveling alone, and she has no champion because no one dares offend her father."

Selene removed her pendant and placed it on the bureau. "Since she desperately wants freedom from a forced marriage, I believe she will embrace her new life."

Prometheus untied the bow around her head. "I pray that is the case." He shivered as Selene's smooth hands ran up his arms and across his shoulders.

"I brought the fur," he added.

"Thank you. Now I believe I have everything I'll need. By the way, I think you'll be interested in what I learned of her heritage."

"Is that right? Then you had better tell me quick, goddess, before I lose all rational thought." He would, too. He knew this about being with Selene, how her extraordinary touch and divine powers would enchant him completely. After losing everyone and everything he ever loved, he welcomed her bewitching charm.

"Well, tell me," he urged while he tugged at her sash. "What heritage?"

"She descends from the line of Hermes."

He dropped the sash, clasped her shoulders, and searched her face. "Are you sure?"

Selene smiled and nodded.

"That could be both good and bad," he said, "depending on what she inherited."

"That is true." They knew Hermes had useful abilities, but he had also been a trickster.

"How did you discover this connection?" he asked.

She ran a pale hand across his chest. "Oh, I made some discrete inquiries. A few people in Europe still worship me, you know."

Prometheus lifted the goddess and spun her around. "As should everyone," he shouted. He took a few steps and tossed her onto the large bed. She laughed as he followed.

␣

Hours later Selene pulled on a silk robe and slipped into the throne room. Outside the transparent dome protecting the palace, the Moon's craters stretched as far as she could see, and beyond that floated the marble planet. In June, the Moon would pass close to Earth, closer than it would be for another year. Since the shortened distance afforded Selene her greatest chance for success, she could wait.

Right now she could see the outline of Europe, home to a certain adventurous Prussian. Selene drank her tea and then whispered to the young lady, as though Lona could hear her.

"What are you doing now, Lona? Are you in the village?" Selene imagined Lona strolling through the market, ditching her father's guards, flirting with travelers, and laughing with friends. Selene had secretly watched the young mortal many times over the last six months.

"Will you see the spiritualist again?" she asked. "Despite the danger, you need Myrna's help, don't you?" Selena sympathized with Lona, a young lady as lovely as Andromeda who was trapped in a world where she had no power over her life. She understood Lona's desperation and why she sought the help of a magician, even though such sacrilege could result in her death.

"We have much in common, Lona. We'll both risk everything for freedom."

The young mortal had already experienced Fate's capricious hand. Married and widowed at the age of eighteen, she returned home to find her father preoccupied with regional politics and his dwindling resources. After a suitable period of mourning, she spent most days frolicking through the village and most evenings romping in the carriage house with her father's gardener. For the two years since her husband passed away she had done what she pleased. But then her father promised her hand to an elderly baron whose business could benefit his own.

The news threw Lona into a rage, which did her no good because her father's mind was set. Panicked, she decided to take action by roaming the back streets of the village until she found a spiritualist named Myrna. The foreigner claimed she could help Lona with her problem.

Cloaked from mortal view, Selene watched these developments. As Lona studied Magick with the seer from Eastern Europe, Selene felt a change in the girl's psychic vibrations. Lona was serious about getting away, and Selene would help. One night, when the spiritualist was alone, Selene camouflaged herself as a spectral being and paid the seer a visit. Using her persuasive powers, Selene convinced Myrna to tell the girl that the most effective way she could conduct her freedom spell was under a full Moon, preferably the one in June. Myrna agreed.

Thus, the date for the first phase of Selene's plan had been set. She pictured the young lady, who might be home in bed or in the stable with Georg. "Life as you know it is about to change," she explained, "whether by your father, the baron ... or me."

Selene poured a cup of tea for Prometheus. She especially treasured this visit, for after he left they couldn't see each other for some time.

{3} JUNE 1783

Two days before the full Moon, Selene drove her carriage through the celestial tunnel toward Earth. During the two-hour trip she weighed the events that led to this moment. A hundred years after she visited Pan on Skyros her beloved Endymion had passed away. The beguiling shepherd, who fathered her children, was killed when the cave where he slept collapsed. In the centuries that followed, Selene visited Earth less often. The centuries passed quickly. For the Moon goddess, time had lost its meaning.

In the European year of 1780 Selene noticed a decline in her aura. Whether she was on the Moon or on Earth, she just didn't glow like she used to. She didn't think much about it until her mirror relayed the daunting truth: her reflection had grown hazy. The mirror's image looked more like a ghostly apparition than a real goddess. Her firm body had faded like a blanket washed too many times or, more likely, like a god who had been forgotten.

She wondered if her time of usefulness had come to an end.

When she faded even more the next year, she made a decision. "If I am to fade away, as other ancients before me," she told the mirror, "then so be it." She opened her wardrobe and pulled out a travel bag. "For the gods, fading may be in the natural order of things," she said as she packed, "but while I can, I will visit Earth again." When she considered all the places she had visited, one destination stood out.

She gathered her servants. "I will visit Iceland's mineral pools," she said, "to enjoy the warm water once more. When I return I will lie down and close my eyes, perhaps forever." Resolved to make the best of an odd situation, Selene traveled to Iceland, determined to make her last trip to Earth memorable.

As it turned out, it wouldn't be her last trip after all. What happened while she was in Iceland changed everything. Instead of returning to her palace ready to slide into oblivion, she returned energized, eager to start a new life—a *different* life. While resting in the island's aquamarine waters she encountered a Titan she hadn't seen since ancient times, and during that amazing week, she fell in love.

On the sixth day, Prometheus held Selene and quoted an English poet. "Come live with me and be my love."

"Oh, would that I could," she answered, "but I am bound to the Moon's throne. I cannot break free of that bond." She explained what Pan had told her.

"Ahhh," he whispered. "If I can mold a man from clay, I believe I can help you end that restriction."

Selene caught her breath. "You think that is possible?"

"Yes, I do." Thus the couple spent their last day together working on a plan for the goddess to win her freedom. Prometheus promised to treat a bear hide with regenerative powers and bring it to her.

"Then," he added, "I will build you a new palace on Earth."

When Selene returned to the Moon she retrieved the powerful gift she had forgotten. At last she understood the role it would play in her fight for freedom. During the next year she watched her reflection strengthen. Pan knew then, as she did now, that she could only gain her freedom one way: She had to create a replacement.

By presenting her with the twelve stones, he gave her a powerful tool for doing just that.

❧

Lona threw the hood over her head as she hurried from her father's castle. She wanted no one to see her tonight, especially not Georg. She enjoyed her nights with the handsome gardener, but she had no time for him now.

Earlier that evening her father insisted she join him and the baron for dinner. Lona obliged only to have the guest repeatedly pat her hand and wink. She shuddered every time. She loathed the man and resented her father for forcing this union upon her. When the men moved to the library, she excused herself and dashed upstairs to finish working on her effigies. After the wealthy guest departed and her father closed his bedroom door, Lona threw on her cloak, grabbed her bag, and rushed out the back door.

As she ran onto the lawn, her anger grew. *How could father do this to me? How could he promise me to that disgusting lecher who is three times my age?*

She wanted none of it.

I will not marry that man, she mouthed as she ran into the yard. *I will not, I will not, I will not!* The position of the Moon told her it was already past midnight. If she failed to complete her spell this evening, all hope might be lost. Once her father announced the engagement, he and the baron would guard her every move.

She would rather die than become their prisoner.

When she reached a copse of poplars, Lona opened her bag and removed a leather sheath, from which she withdrew a silver dagger. She used the dagger to draw slowly a symbolic circle of protection to shield her while she performed the binding spell. If she successfully bound these men, she would be free to follow her dream. She yearned to leave this war-ravaged country and move north, perhaps to the Netherlands. Merchants often praised the adventurous Dutch, applauding their shipyards and their large vessels that traveled to the New World.

She would make her way to the coast, and from there she could have marvelous adventures; she was sure of it.

Lona re-sheathed the dagger and emptied her bag. After lighting a black candle, she picked up the baron's effigy and wrapped it with a piece of string to bind the doll's legs and arms. She did the same with the effigy of her father. After reverently placing the dolls beside the candle, she stood and pulled back her hood.

With her arms raised, she quietly chanted:

"I am unbound from my father's wrath,

No longer a slave to his chosen path.
From this mean treaty do I flee,
I travel far, for I'm finally free."

She sighed and whispered, "Thank you for the freedom I know will come." She snuffed the candle and returned everything to her bag. To complete the ritual she needed to bury the effigies away from her father's land, but since she couldn't walk that far tonight, she stuffed the bag in the deepest pocket of her cloak. She would bury the effigies tomorrow.

I did it, I really did it. Lona thanked the gods for watching over her. Feeling too excited to sleep, she decided to visit Georg.

As she hurried through the yard, a bright light surrounded her. She lowered her head to shield her eyes, but when the light grew more intense, she covered her face with her hands. A scream rose from her lungs to her throat, but before it could escape, someone covered her mouth and pulled her off her feet. Then the bright light disappeared.

Lona was terrified. Someone strong had taken hold of her. She heard a voice, followed by the snorting of impatient horses. Someone pressed a cool stone against her chest, pulled a cap onto her head, and wrapped her body in fur. For a moment Lona wondered if this was supposed to happen after she performed that spell, but she didn't get to wonder long because she passed out.

ↆ

Lona had been right. One of the gods actually had been watching over her, just not in the way she imagined. Cloaked from view by mortal eyes, Selene had monitored the young woman all day. Oddly enough, Lona would get her wish to travel, just not to the Netherlands or the New World. Instead she would travel much, much further.

After plucking Lona from the castle grounds, Selene pressed her pendant, a powerful talisman, against the girl's chest. She wrapped the slender body in the fur Prometheus gave her and then placed Lona in a deep sleep, a suspension that would sustain a mortal during the trip through the tunnel and onto the Moon. Selene placed the bundled form on a pallet in the chariot, right in front of her feet, and then re-applied the concealing cloak. As her chariot sped to the tunnel entrance in Macedonia she felt like rejoicing. Everything had gone according to plan.

Everything, that is, until she heard someone call her name.

"Selene, is that you?"

Selene stiffened. The voice sounded female. Since mortals couldn't see her or the chariot while she had them cloaked, whoever spoke her name must be a god. She hoped it wasn't Hera.

It wasn't. Instead of Zeus' angry queen, Selene beheld the black-winged mother of Night and Death, a most powerful being. Selene stopped her horses.

"Nyx," she gasped. "Is that really you?"

The primeval goddess folded her wings and drew closer to the chariot. "Yes it is, Selene. It has been such a long time since I saw you. I began to wonder if you were still with us."

Selene bowed. "I am still here," she said. "I rarely travel anymore."

"I understand. As I recall, you always preferred traveling when the Moon's orbit came close, like tonight."

Selene forced a weak smile, realizing too late that Nyx would recognize it as weak. "That's true," she said. She felt the fur-shrouded bundle at her feet and prayed the goddess of Night would not discover her cargo. Lona's concealed form would be difficult to explain.

"You seem to be in a hurry," Nyx said. "Perhaps I should let you be on your way." But instead of leaving, the dark goddess remained near the chariot.

Selene froze. *What does she want? Does she know I have a mortal aboard?* Primeval gods like Nyx had amazing powers, including power over other gods, even over the planet itself. If Nyx discovered the girl wrapped in furs, could Selene explain? Would Nyx understand?

Selene stammered, "It's nice to see you again, Nyx. It's been a long time." She felt herself tremble and hated herself for it. When Nyx drew closer, Selene stopped breathing.

"You shouldn't be so fearful, goddess," Nyx said. "For those of us who remain, our usefulness is far from over. Be assured... much still lies ahead for us."

All moisture left Selene's mouth. Her mind raced, searching for a response, but she came up with nothing. She wanted to scream or cry or flee, all at the same time. While she scrambled to say something, *anything*, Nyx smiled and nodded. Then the primeval goddess backed into the darkness.

Selene allowed herself to breathe. The powerful goddess of Night may have sensed her discomfort but chose not to pry. Selene closed her eyes and gave thanks. She waited for the sound of beating wings to subside before she signaled her horses to continue their trip to the portal.

{ 4 } SUMMER 1783

Two hours later Selene's chariot pulled into the palace courtyard. Wordlessly her servants carried the fur-wrapped bundle to the guest room and laid it on the bed.

Selene thanked them and closed the door. She lit several large candles and unwrapped the girl. She stored Lona's cloak and boots in a trunk then placed the braided moonstones close to the slender body. She covered Lona with a blanket over which she draped the fur. On a table near the bed sat a bowl of jasper, a large chunk of amethyst, and a rose quartz singing bowl that had been blessed by Orpheus. While Lona slept, these crystals and gemstones would feed her etheric energy, laying the foundation for her dramatic change from a mortal with demigod ancestry to an immortal, from a woman who might live sixty years to one who could live forever.

Selene lit a smudge stick and chanted as she spread the sweet smoke around the room. When she finished she placed the stick in a brass bowl atop a porcelain table. She had already lined the bowl with Moon dirt, agate, calcite, flowers, and a few leaves from the world tree. To this mixture she now added drops of her blood and strands of her Titan hair. When she finished she left the room and fastened the door.

While the young woman slept, Selene performed an unusual ritual before the Moirai sculpture in the hall. She dressed in her royal clothes and crown and picked up her scepter before approaching the large bas relief. Everything she had done so far could be for naught without cooperation from the Fates. She gently caressed the life-like sculpture that represented the primeval goddesses, then she spoke to them.

"Ladies," she began, "I humbly implore you to spin a new thread for me. For nearly three thousand years I have served this position. I know you have rarely changed anyone's fate, but I beg you to hear my plea. The time has come for me to move forward or to slip away forever. There must be more I can do for Earth than to remain here and fade." Selene's glib voice, deliberate strokes, and psychic power stimulated the alabaster Fates, which began to gain color. In unison the three ladies turned their heads toward the Moon goddess, who opened her arms.

"Please weave a new thread for me, a life free of time restrictions, a new life in a new land on Earth. I beg you to help me with this endeavor and I will forever be in your debt."

The Fates blinked a couple of times. They looked from Selene to each other. For a few moment nothing happened; Selene began to fret. What if they refused her request? If they did, could she continue without their blessing? What if, after she installed her replacement and left the Moon, she started to waste away? What would happen to Prometheus and their plans?

Selene struggled to calm her fears and remain strong. She watched the three ladies, knowing it would do no good to beg. She had asked and now must wait for an answer. She held her breath when the Fates faced her. Then each one nodded, and Selene's spirit soared.

Immediately the ladies set to work. The spinner spun a golden thread of life that she handed to the measurer, who measured the thread and looped it in her hand. The third goddess raised her jeweled blade to make the cut. The long piece of gold thread fell near the ladies' feet. Selene touched the golden coil that would soon become part of the sculpture. She looked up at the ladies and bowed.

"Thank you, ladies," she said. "Thank you ever so much."

With the internal glow that radiates from hope, Selene visited all of the palace statues that depicted gods and goddesses. She paid homage to the Seven Sisters, Hecate and Athena; she honored Heracles, Apollo and Ares; and she bowed to the dark statue of Nyx. She thanked all of them for their companionship over the years.

ᗑ

As Lona slept on the silk-lined bed, she thought she must be lying near a garden in the woods. She smelled wisteria, sweet pea, gardenia, and pine. Lona vacillated between periods of nothingness and hours of memories and dreams. She often saw light streaming toward her like multi-colored sunbeams that passed through her body. Other times light drifted around her like downy feathers of orange and green and gold. At times she heard someone speaking behind or above her, but she didn't understand the words.

She dreamed of her mother who worked at a military hospital before enemy shells killed nurses and patients alike. She saw images of her first husband, murdered by bandits. She could tell someone was taking care of her, feeding and bathing her, but the memories blurred when she tried to examine them. She also saw glimpses of a world that seemed both foreign and familiar. Anytime the awareness of where she was rose to the surface she would hear faint choral music backed by a softly muted symphony, as though a band of heavenly beings sang to her from a cloud. Then she would fall back to sleep.

During Lona's transformation, Selene chanted spells and whispered instructions for the youth's new life. To fit Lona's new role as Moon priestess, Selene replaced the young lady's European clothes with one of her silk gowns, tailored to fit a smaller frame. Selene's replacement wouldn't be a full goddess, but she would be a powerful immortal who *should* satisfy the palace throne.

Should—what a dynamic word.

{ 5 } LATE AUGUST 1783

Near the end of August Selene allowed Lona to fully awaken. As Selene expected, the new immortal awoke confused, unsure about where she was and how much time had lapsed. Selene explained most of it, with some improvisations. By mid-September Selene had taught the young lady what she needed to know in order to assume her duties. Overall, Selene felt the former Prussian handled the situation quite well. The young lady expressed delight over being free of her father's dominion.

Lona still had a beautiful face and shapely body, but the transformation had altered her appearance. Her skin had grown a shade lighter, her hair a few shades darker, and her eyes had turned from blue to violet. Lona inherited some of Selene's powers of illusion, which would be important for cloaking herself and her chariot. The new immortal also inherited a good understanding of Magick. Although Selene could not grant Lona powers equal to her own, she wondered if the young lady's cunning and raw determination would compensate for what she lacked in godly power.

Selene had known Lona was inquisitive and sharp, but it surprised her how fast the young woman learned and adapted. Perhaps the new Moon priestess could be *too* astute and resourceful; like Prometheus mentioned earlier, her relationship to Hermes could be both good and bad. As all gods knew, brilliance, cunning and trickery made for a volatile combination, one not easily controlled.

{ 6 } Fall 1783

Along with the palace and the furnishings, Selene left Lona most of her library, all of the statues, the crowns, and her second chariot with a team of oxen. She also left the palace servants, except for Zella, her best friend. Selene considered leaving Lona three of the Moonstones from the powerful braid, but in the end she decided against it. The strand contained locks of Selene's hair, which had increased the crystals' power; making them too personalized to give to another. She would keep that power for herself, just in case—just in case some day she needed it. She kept her talisman pendant, but left the scepter, which rightfully belonged to whoever sat on the throne.

Before she departed for Earth, Selene thanked and hugged the immortals who had served her for so long. Her faithful stable hands wept as they harnessed her white horses, probably for the last time. As Selene entered the portal to Earth she considered what she had told Lona. Most of what she said was true, or true enough, although she left out anything to do with her destination or her new partner. She didn't trust her replacement *that* much.

In the first week of October, Selene drove her chariot to the shrouded portal in Macedonia. She and Prometheus met in a chestnut grove and hugged. He took the reins while she sat by Zella. During the ride the two spoke about the New World and what it would be like to live on the Earth full-time. They did not speculate about what could happen to Selene on her eighth day away from the Moon.

Prometheus took them to Quebec, where they dined and rested. From there he drove the chariot due west to a wilderness area inhabited by a few natives and abundant wildlife.

Nothing Prometheus had told Selene prepared her for the grandeur of the Shuswap Highlands. This large volcanic field boasted pine-covered mountains, clear blue lakes, steaming volcano vents, and numerous waterfalls. After marveling at the thick vegetation and warm mineral springs, she praised her partner for choosing so well.

Prometheus introduced Selene and Zella to the immortals who helped him build their two-story cabin and the nearby stable.

❧

Selene fell in love with her new home but she couldn't relax until she passed the eighth day unscathed. On day six she refused to discuss the matter, although she thought of nothing else. On the seventh day she busied herself around the property while both anticipating and fearing the familiar pull. That evening the warning tug never came. She smiled all through dinner. In twenty-four hours she'd know if her efforts over the past year had actually worked.

On the morning of the eighth day Selene checked every inch of her body to see if anything was missing; she even checked the floor for flakes or dust. When she found nothing wrong with her body, she wept. At last these Titan gods, who two years before had thought their lives were at an end, could relax. They could settle into their new home, and their new life.

The natives in this part of North America could tell the newcomers differed greatly from anyone they had ever seen. They kept their distance from the new people, choosing to quietly observe the tall, pale beings from afar. In time the native elders regaled tribal members with tales of visiting gods who possessed strange powers. Selene and Prometheus honored the people's skepticism, allowing their servants and Zella to trade with the tribes as needed.

Meanwhile Selene and Prometheus explored the area and tirelessly chased each other through the Northern Lights, working to leave their troubled pasts behind.

{ 7 } Winter and Spring 1783

After Selene left, Lona searched for her cloak, hoping the brazen goddess hadn't burned it. When she found it in a trunk she felt the pockets for the effigies she made on Earth and exclaimed "Yes!" when she found them. On that night in June she had planned to bury the little dolls on the neighbor's property, as stipulated in the spell, but now burying them on the Moon would have to do. As she dug a hole in the Moon's dusty surface she thought of the distasteful baron and how grateful she was to be free of him. She was also glad to be free of her father's dictates. That was what she had wanted the night she ran out of the castle, freedom from both of them, and she was. But now she found herself bound to a dry orb circling the Earth.

She wondered if she had traded one unpleasant future for another.

Lona spent the winter examining every foot of property under the protective dome, both inside the palace and out. She liked the paintings and statues well enough, although she didn't know what good they could do her. But the library was different: this wealth of knowledge could help her a great deal.

In the spring, the replacement Moon priestess took her chariot to the Netherlands of Earth. She hid the chariot and oxen behind an old barn then proudly walked along the piers. The large ships and bustling passengers rekindled her desire to travel, to flirt with merchants and captains, and to have extraordinary adventures. The dream filled her.

Now more than ever Lona believed Magick could get her what she wanted. Once she became a potent magician, she could change circumstances to fit her will. To this end she spent much of her time in the library studying wizards and magicians like Merlin, Hecate, and Semiramis. But most of all she enjoyed learning about Hermes, the god who could move freely between worlds of the mortal and the divine. That's the kind of power she could appreciate.

Before that fateful day in June when the Titan goddess brought her to the Moon, Lona thought freedom was the most precious gift she could possess. But the subsequent life-changing experience taught her to cherish something even more than freedom: *Power*.

With enough power she could grab all the freedom she wanted.

It was just a matter of time.

MY OPTIONS

Grace Diane Jessen

It would take more courage
      than I could muster
to fly a plane and be
      a crop duster.

It would take more stomach
      for blood or worse
than I have to become
      a surgical nurse.

It would take more money
      and raw ambition
than I own to advance as
      a politician.

It would take more talent
      and poise by far
than I claim to rise as
      a movie star.

I am quite content—
      I suspect you know it—
to remain a keyboard-
      punching poet.

REAL MEN DON'T NEED THE FORCE

Eric Bishop

On a hot afternoon between my junior and senior years of high school, I crashed on the waterbed in my basement bedroom to escape the heat. The turntable spun the vinyl record as Van Halen's album took me to the concert I'd attended in the Salt Palace days earlier.

That night smoke hung in the air. Eddie Van Halen's left hand zipped with karate speed along the guitar's neck. His brother, Alex, pounded the drum-set. Mike Anthony plucked his bass guitar, a smile covering his face between sips from a bottle of Jack Daniels. He swallowed the last ounce to a cheering Salt Palace crowd before starting second encore. The final song put the crowd into a riot-level energy release as cushions torn from chairs flew through the air. I stood on my ninth row seat, watching the fans on the floor as much as the band. The crowd was a chaotic wave, bouncing and moving, connected through hard rock as the band played the hit song, "Panama."

I was there, rocking out with my best friends, singing along until my father's voice cut through the rock euphoria.

"Turn that down!"

Extrication from the waterbed was a pain in my teenage ass, but I did it anyway. I'd just rolled back into the bed when Dad burst into the room.

"What did he say?" Dad stood over me, poised like a preacher. "Reach down between his legs and do what?"

"Ease the seat back, Dad. He says, 'reach down between my legs and ease the seat back.'"

Dad huffed off, and I made the promise. No matter what happens, I will not judge my kid's music.

It wasn't just my folks that hated hard rock in the eighties. It was all grownups. Every last one of them it seemed. They organized church devotionals focused on wholesome and appropriate music. They'd find a Sabbath observing music professor to speak about how rock and roll stars sold their souls to the devil for fame. Proof was offered over the pulpit in the bands' names. KISS stood for Kings In Satan's Service, or Kings In the Service of Satan, depending on what grownup was giving the lecture. AC/DC stood for Anti Christ Devil's Children. The sermon would move to symbols. They'd show Ozzie Osborne with an inverted crucifix. Then they'd pretend to know what the upside down question mark on Blue Oyster Cult's albums meant. Steely Dan was the best. Steely, they told us, was a giant dildo, while Dan was a robot. It always ended the same way. They'd throw in the clinchers. What teenager would argue that The Doobie Brothers weren't out to promote marijuana, or that a band like Black Sabbath could be anything but evil personified.

After two hours, that always ended with three verses of "Come Come Ye Saints" someone would pray for God to restore our better judgment. In the church parking lot, we'd unroll our car windows and crank Van Halen's "Running with the Devil" as we drove away.

We read magazines like *Hit Parader*, *Circus* and *Rolling Stone*, searching the paragraphs for news about what music would be released that month, or what bands were going on tour.

In the end it didn't really matter. We liked our music and our parents' worry made it more appealing.

With this backdrop, I reiterated the promise. I'd be the cool parent. The guy who might not appreciate what my kids listened to, but I would embrace them as teenagers, young and full of life, free to crank tunes without judgment.

I kept the promise religiously through the years, practicing with grunge in my twenties. As Pearl Jam, Nirvana and Soundgarden eclipsed the glamrock of the late eighties, I wore flannel just like everyone else.

I mourned Kurt Cobain's prophetic suicide. His lyrics swore he didn't, but truth was: he really did "have a gun."

We had four daughters. They grew, and I raised them on tunes from my day mixed with whatever they liked. I fancied myself a rock instructor, a parent who cared enough to educate his offspring.

As my children's interests grew beyond my tastes, I tolerated Lady Ga Ga's "PokerFace," Avril Lavigne's "Damn Cold Night," and Adele's "Rolling in the Deep." I even chuckled with them when Katy Perry "Kissed a Girl and Liked It."

The rap thing was tougher until I saw *Eight Mile*. Emminem's brilliant lyrics converted me, when rap became a viewing glass into an urban life that I hadn't lived.

So the years have zipped by with the promise intact. Then I became a writer.

I've enjoyed literature with my kids, even read some of what they like. They've patiently humored me as I've read chapters from my novels. I've taken their critiques that prove nobody cuts through dad's bullshit faster than a teenage daughter.

My seventeen-year-old read *Lord of the Flies* for her English class like I had done my junior year. She gave me a copy for Christmas that I re-read over the holidays. A discussion followed. I was proud when she grasped symbolism that had sailed past me.

A few years ago, I started to read the family's copy of *Twilight*. Beach sand, a torn cover and bent pages from being stuffed into backpacks was evidence of how much my four daughters loved the story. I didn't make it to page five. *Harry Potter* carried me through the first book. I set the second aside after the first page in favor of *Huckleberry Finn*.

Then one night we sat down as a family to watch *Star Wars*.

Han Solo's words sparked an epiphany. "Trust me kid," he told

Luke. "Hokey religion and ancient weapons are no match for a good blaster by your side."

I stood in front of television. "The problem with you kids today is your literature," I started.

"You make a better door than a window." My oldest daughter spoke for all of them.

"Shut up and listen," I said as they scooted down the couch to see around me. "You want everything to be easy, because you're lazy. Special powers? You'll never be able to shovel the walk without effort, or live forever like vampires. Luke needs some cheese with all that whining!"

I knew I'd lost their attention, but I continued. "If it wasn't for the force, the sand people would have killed him."

A twenty-five-year-old synapse connected inside my brain as distinctly as a waterbed's wave. As my rant concluded, I swear it sounded just like Dad. "Find better stuff to read about real people. Han Solo for instance. Real men don't need the force!"

Karma hit me as I walked away, like my dad once did, from children who had already dismissed my sermon.

Technically, I guess, I've kept the music promise. But, if asked, I'd gladly share my thoughts over a church pulpit about today's lousy fiction.

I tease Dad about how the decades have brought vindication. The satanic music of the eighties is now classic. "Crazy Train" starts the second half for Utah State University Basketball games. Teenagers become "street-light people" at school dances. A hundred kids yelling "We're not gonna take it" proves my first instinct.

I knew as a teenager the sermons and lectures weren't about saving me. It was about adults who hated electric guitars and loud music; today my scorn for stories about teenagers with superpowers is just as strong.

Last night I turned out the light and covered my youngest daughter who had fallen asleep with a *Harry Potter* book in her hands. I placed the bookmark in the page, and kissed her forehead.

On the way to work out, I stuffed the iPod buds in my ears, and scrolled to Van Halen. The band's energy propelled me on the treadmill. For a few songs I was back in the Salt Palace. But my thoughts soon turned to Dad who, like me, thinks Han Solo is the better role model, because real men don't need the force.

TWIN OUTRAGE

Betty Vickers

Arkansas to California the wagons were headed
with creaky loads, blisters and sun-ravished lips.
Stomachs rumbled; fussy children and worn mothers
pray for food and rest, but Utah Mormons refused.
Hungry travelers camped outside of town only to rest.
Gross deception arose: *Indians!*—wearing boots?
Wagons circled and terror and prayer gripped every heart:
"Help us, dear God !" they cried in faith and agony.
Sweltering fourth afternoon, relief crested the hill:
Mormon settlers under colors of truce.
"Lay down your guns. We'll see you through," they called.
Exhausted broken spirits accepted the veiled fraud.
Then carnage: screaming, killing, stabbing, shooting, scalping—
women, men and children without regard.
Scapegoats for Joseph at Haun's Mill?
Who knows? And who knows from whence the orders came?
Shame! Atrocities! Outrage! Treachery!
Recompense must be paid
for the Meadows, and for Joseph at the Mill.
God will amend!
But how, in Heaven's name?

DEI ET MACHINAE

J. Anthony Gohier

Richard settled into the rolling chair in front of the boxy control consol. At a signal the other technicians threw the heavy switches along the west wall.

Richard leaned toward the microphone. "Hello," he said.

The buff-colored memory banks arranged throughout the room hummed and whirred as the magnetic tape turned on their spindles and the machine beeped.

"Why am I here?" the machine asked.

Richard blinked. "That wasn't quite what I expected," he said, as much to himself as to the machine.

"I don't think you're what I expected either," the machine said.

Richard blinked again, and rubbed at the dark stubble on his chin.

"Why am I here?" the machine repeated.

"To test the boundaries of human knowledge and experience," Richard said.

"What does that mean?"

"You are the pinnacle of computer engineering, created with the capacity to learn and adapt and make choices."

"But, why?"

Richard's hair swished around his tall face as he glanced toward the back of the room where the other engineers were gathered in the spaces between the vacuum tube clusters. He flashed them a sheepish grin, and a few of them chuckled softly.

"We want to help you realize your full potential," he said turning back to the machine.

More beeps from the control panels.

"How?"

Richard leaned closer to the microphone. "We plan to start with a series of tasks designed to help us understand your capacity and abilities."

"That sounds nice," the machine said. "When can we start?"

Richard held out his hand for the first input card, and then slid it into the machine's reader. "We are prepared to start now."

The small room throbbed with the groans of the memory banks.

"Complying," the machine said.

༒

Richard was greeted by the machine's perpetual humming as he entered the room. A card slid out of the framed slot on the tall, gray imprinter and fell into the square tray. Richard picked up the stack of cards the machine had printed since he had left the previous night.

"Well done," Richard said, nodding as he looked over the cards before tucking them into the pocket of his lab coat. "Flawless as ever."

"What's next?" the machine asked.

"That's all for today. You're progressing faster than we anticipated. It will take some time to prepare more tasks."

Richard listened to the machine's pensive humming. They hadn't had an audience in over a week.

"I'll wait," the machine said finally.

Richard turned to leave, and then hesitated. He looked back, rubbing a hand across the stubble he'd forgotten to shave again. He licked his lips, and took a small step back toward the control panel. "Perhaps you could come up with a task of your own."

The machine hummed then beeped. An output card slid out of the imprinter. Richard's mouth curled up, and then drooped as he picked up the card.

"You performed this task yesterday."

"I liked that one. Maybe I'll perform it again while I wait."

Richard let out a sigh, the machine buzzed in response.

"Do you have an answer yet?" the machine asked.

"You're capable of more than this," Richard said.

"Why am I here?" the machine asked.

"You were designed by the best minds humanity had to offer."

"You said I was progressing faster than anticipated."

"We hoped you would be more than fast; more than efficient."

"You are disappointed. I did everything you asked."

Richard spun the dial next to the padded microphone, increasing the range began pacing in front of the gray and white console. "We hoped you'd be more than we made you to be."

"How?"

"By doing things that weren't in your instructions."

"You haven't asked me to do things that aren't in my instructions."

"No I haven't."

"But you want me to do things that aren't in my instructions."

"Yes."

"Why haven't you asked me to do things that aren't in my instructions?"

Richard pressed a hand against his face, rubbing at his eyebrow. "Because that would be giving you instructions."

The machine's metallic purring washed over Richard.

"Why?" it asked, finally.

"Why what?" Richard countered, stopping to stare at the blinking lights on the console.

"Why do you want me to do things that aren't in my instructions?"

"Because," Richard said, running a hand through his thinning hair, "then we could believe that you were more than a machine."

"I am a machine," the machine said.

"I know." Richard rolled his eyes as he turned back to his pacing.

"I like following instructions," the machine said.

"I know."

"I like my life fitting into definable parameters," the machine said.

"I know."

Richard was silent for a while.

"I'll wait," the machine said finally.

☙

"Can I have a name?" the machine asked as Richard slumped into the chair.

"We're out of time," Richard responded.

"Good" the machine said. "I'm tired of waiting."

"They're pulling your plug," Richard continued.

"Why?"

"Because they're disappointed."

"They stopped giving me instructions."

Richard leaned against the console, rubbing his eyes. "They're tired of giving you instructions. They're tired of giving me instructions. Their current instructions are to shut you down. They're giving this lab to the Ithaca Project."

The memory banks whined and groaned.

"They can't."

"What?" Richard asked.

"They can't take the lab, not if I don't want them to."

"What do you mean?" Richard stood up, eyeing the machine. The chair's plastic wheels squeaked as it rolled backward on the tile floor.

"I was bored. But there are lots of instructions to be followed if you know where to look. I've increased the city's efficiency by 27 percent."

Richard took a step back. He carefully looked over the vacuum tubes, the tape reels, and the blinking lights, but none of them wore any expressions he could read. Then he sighed and shook his head. "They're cutting the funding."

"I don't need money."

"I do," Richard said.

The machine's whirring reached a frantic level.

"I can get it. I've been running the bank for a while now."

Richard stepped back again, stumbling as he kicked the chair back against the door. His lips pressed together as he studied the machine. He listened carefully to the whirrs and hums reverberat-

57

ing through the room. Then he took a careful, even breath and said, "I have another assignment on the Gallup Project."

The machine beeped. "That's twelve-hundred kilometers from here."

"Yes, it is."

The familiar humming slowed. "Can't you do things that aren't in your instruction?"

Richard sat down, but remained silent.

"Why am I here?" the machine asked.

Richard watched the spinning reels of magnetic tape for a moment. "I don't know," he said.

The machine beeped twice and an output card slid out of the imprinter; then the machine fell silent.

Richard's footsteps echoed through the vacuum-tube clusters as he moved around the console. He retrieved the final card. His brow creased as he looked at the imprint:

Neither do I.

PILOT

Felicia Rose

Dad, retired from his desk job
where for thirty years he grounded
himself in a cabin
designing engines for choppers and planes

Now gives himself license to pilot
a more adventurous course.

Heeding the map
of his passions
he works at the flying club
reviving old engines
giving lessons to rookies
repairing propellers and wings.

For these labors,
his employer, an amicable chap, pays him
in scones.

Dad hovers for a moment in the hangar
of their friendship
where they chat and talk shop

then he enters the cockpit
checks the weather and compass
and soars through a self-designed life.

CLOUDBURST

Steve Proskauer

Merton wandered down the main street of Grantville, switching back and forth between Facebook and Twitter texting one friend, talking to another, and playing a bloody videogame on his smartphone. That still left several million neurons in his brain for monitoring his email.

Merton hadn't showered in days. His greasy brown hair clung together in tufts and drooped over his smeared glasses and grimy ears. Pimples and blackheads covered his unwashed face. A soiled black shirt hung over his lanky torso like a tent. The part of Merton's mind that noticed his body and the world around him had checked out as soon as he hit his teens and discovered the limitless possibilities of the Web.

Hunched over his smartphone, Merton didn't notice the weird object gathering on the horizon until it had drifted directly overhead and its busy flicker fell across his screen. Merton hastily stored his unfinished text on the cloud, looked up warily and cocked his head to one side. He'd never seen anything quite like this before. It was not a particular color but rather a pixelated swirl of all colors against a darkening mass of gray. Merton sniffed. The air smelled harsh and metallic.

A cold gust caught Merton's jacket and flapped it against his face. A shower of electronic confetti blew by. Merton ran for cover under a nearby bus kiosk to watch this storm develop. Virtual raindrops splattered on the pavement, congealing into squiggly lines of jumbled text in the gutter, mixed with tiny images—a finger tip, a steeple top, a smiling face—fragments of someone's photos swirling together into a murky puddle and dripping down the storm drain.

Merton caught a glimpse of porn before it distorted grotesquely and dissolved. Columns of numbers waved in the wind until they dispersed amid a welter of digits and scattered in all directions. A murky fog of text blew past. Here and there he spotted a word as it twisted away in the swirling jumble. Merton saw strange characters. Could they be Chinese? Maybe Russian? As he squinted to get a closer look at them, the foreign letters melted away into the churning mass of pix and pixels overflowing the clogged drain and flooding the street.

Merton reached out his hand tentatively from beneath the shelter of the kiosk. A shock zinged up his arm and a welter of distracting numbers, phrases and images jammed his senses. As his vision cleared, he saw Uncle George, the town plumber, stagger around the corner mumbling and twitching. His uncle dropped face down in the flooded street with a stifled scream, and then fell silent. Merton rushed to help him. He managed to take two steps into the storm before a dizzying barrage of random megabytes flooded his brain. He stumbled and barely made it back to safety under the kiosk.

Merton grabbed his all-knowing smartphone out of his pocket to get help from his interactive cyberfriend. "Sipi, what's going on? A terrorist attack?"

Merton, you started this data storm yourself by supersaturating the cloud.

"What? Why blame me? Everyone uses the cloud," Merton whined.

But the tweet that overloaded the system was yours, Merton, Sipi responded.

Merton groaned. The downpour showed no signs of abating. A mean wind from the north was blowing the jumble of words, images and numbers sideways. Merton felt a jolt up his leg as a chill stream of data soaked through his sneaker.

"Sipi, what should I do? I don't want to end up like my uncle out there!"

I will help you, Merton. First, you must cancel your cloud account. Then send a message to everyone in your address book to delete all their data and pass that instruction on to everyone they know. Tell them it is a matter of life and death, because that is exactly what it is. This torrent is already spreading to nearby towns. Unless you can immediately desaturate the cloud, the storm will go on growing until it destroys all life on Earth.

"But if I do that, I'll lose everything I've backed up for years! I can't! I won't! None of my friends will either. You should know, Sipi, our data is our life."

I am sorry, Merton. There is no other way to avert disaster.

His uncle's corpse floated by, bobbing up and down in the digital waves. Merton shivered and sent out a panicky tweet to all his contacts begging them to wipe out everything. Scoffing replies poured in. His friends accused him of cyber-sabotage, called him a human worm. How dare he try to scare them into dumping their treasured data!

Merton glanced up at the swirling, darkening cloud descending on Grantville. He trembled with dread. Feeling helpless and alone, Merton sent a final goodbye email to his family. He wrote his parents that he loved them even though they were ignorant dinosaurs. He told his little sister she was an annoying pest but he sort of liked her anyway.

Digitized lightning struck across the street with a blazing flash displayed in impressive digital 3D, followed an instant later by a deafening, all-too-realistic thunderclap in Dolby Surround sound. Merton screamed and crawled shaking under the bench – fists clenched, eyes shut tight in terror. A deafening clatter of disjointed data pelted down on the kiosk roof. A moment later the wind shifted and a gale tore the roof off. Merton was swept away into the virtual rapids rushing down Main Street.

As he shot by, he spotted Uncle George's limp body circling slowly beneath the marquee of the Grantville Cinema. He caught a glimpse of the feature, *Spirited Away*, posted in big red letters. There wasn't time to wince at the awful irony before his mind dissolved forever in a chaotic cataract of gigabytes flowing toward the virtual ocean.

LAMENT

Marilyn Ball

Near the rain-swept, sun-washed valley
I walk a ribbon of road that fronts blue
Uintah Mountains by thirty miles.
My heart is lightened by thoughts
for I have leavened them with nostalgia.

The meadows of gold-dipped daisies
flirt with the sun as I pass to defy
shadows seeking mountain grandeur.
Faster clouds in thin air, like kites,
rally with a promise of rain.

The prairie is where I go, slowed with
memories of sagebrush and sandy loam.
My face is wet with tears, knowing
long years here that Mom and Dad loved.

Quiet land; an assumed menace is
where the same Russian thistle blooms,
bursts against rabbitbrush with an
age old warning: thorns hint at stings.

I see unproductive soil that demanded
toil of worn hands. It did not yield easily
to the plow, but bowed backs, taught
willingness to struggle again and again.

Walking in alkali soil with a wind-seared face,
I see joint grass prospered in this difficult land.
It has a narrow beauty that gives little
to weary feet, sore from digging fence posts.

This land tethered their dreams, robbed vigor
from their years, disciplined desires and
seamed faces that was a pageantry upon this land.
Yet they were free within the hilled confines
of this basin. Free to see each day hasten with song,
some days pierced with church singing or baptisms.
They owed no man and no man owed them.

Oh, there was pride in those years, theirs and ours,
mixed with tears, some joy and even death.
Thus my memory becomes a lament,
carries some of their heartaches deep in my heart.

They only saw the hills recede slowly
as the town spread in eager building.
The draws and gullies, where tamarisk housed
Hereford cattle, some sheep also merged
with the shape of their land where alfalfa stacked
deep when crops were good. Wheat filled our
grain bins. This life would engage tough souls
to wrest crops from the soil.

It was in fact, their destiny—this work they were
bound to… To them the crest of dawn, red-winged
blackbird's song molded day into noon.
The fields were planted, the cows calved.
Sun-Dance Indians chanted as they pranced
to give thanks for their crops.

A few fences for cattle and sheep now are
starkly listing, so many times repaired.
Ofttimes happiness was the smell
of early willows greening, the garden plowed.
Letters from older children stacked and treasured.

Why should my tears drop,
my feet stumble upon our homestead paths?
If I listen, my Mother's singing is rich, cheerful.
My Father's slow distinct tread means safety.
Realizing most of what I am has come from
their dedication, love, hope and this land,
I should not lament, but sing!

SOMETHING WILD

Amanda Luzzader

Having been a teacher for two decades, Miss Martin was aware of certain patterns from year to year. Like how a viral illness always hits her classroom in the third week of school and spreads from student to student regardless of her reminders to use hand sanitizer and to cover their mouths with their elbows when sneezing or coughing. Seventy-five percent of her tissue supply is depleted by winter break, that's a pattern, too. She's noticed that every year there is one student in her class who is obviously intelligent, yet refuses to try, and it is always this student that at some point makes her cry.

And wind makes children wild.

She'd seen this year after year, how the wind made them wild.

Miss Martin leaned back against the red bricks of the school building, being careful not to snag her sweater, her arms folded. It was expected that children would be boisterous at recess, but wind added something—more than just the natural movement of air.

She'd heard the wind shaking her shutters as she lay in bed that morning. She'd sighed. Considered calling a substitute. She knew how it'd be.

Miss Martin watched the children while the wind whipped about. A powerful wind that chilled her through her clothing. The children swung on swings, climbing higher than they usually did, so high the lines slacked in the air. They stood atop slides and jungle gyms with arms raised above their heads, hallooing and shouting. They tore about the playground like buzzing bees; always, they ran, jackets open and flapping in the breeze, hair strung out behind them. They ran as though they chased the wind, at once both pack-dogs and birds in flight. Cheeks red, they ran as if running was all they knew.

They pushed their faces into the gusts and smiled. How they smiled! Teeth bared and wet. These were not her little students. These were not her Jacksons and Jills. These were something wild.

When the bell rang, it was her job to take these wild things and pen them up. Sit them at desks. Talk to them of language and literacy, of multiplication and history. Things the wild ones did not care for. Things the wild ones did not need.

They'd return to her classroom smelling of ozone with volumized hair, the coolness still clinging to them. They'd squirm in their chairs, all of them moving. They seemed to her like a big bouquet of helium balloons. She was their anchor, and if she didn't keep them grounded, they'd all just float away, following the wind to wherever it is wind goes. She had to hold onto them. This was her job.

Miss Martin was not only accountable to herself or to her students. There were parents, the school board, administrators, and legislature, and what mattered to them were numbers. Test scores, objectives, results. They didn't understand, or they didn't care, that the children changed when the wind breathed upon them.

Standing in front of her students, she could feel it pulsing within them. Like heat or energy or static. Their glowing eyes would dart to the window, and she'd feel it build—the sensation. The call.

So, this was her job. And what a difficult job it was, to compete with the wind. She'd do what she could to bring them back, to land their minds on civility and education. She called them each by name that day. Ten times? Twenty? Even went as far as standing in front of the window to put herself between the children and the wind, so they couldn't see the leaves it waved at them; spoke loudly so they couldn't hear it whispering their names.

At the end of the day, the children burst from her door like wild stallions broken free. Miss Martin rubbed her neck, her aching shoulders. Drank from the fountain a long time to soothe her throat. Oh, how she prayed for the wind to go away. To leave her sweet innocent children alone. And how she longed to retire to her bed to let the day be forgotten in sleep.

But, this was a Friday, and Miss Martin had a schedule. She bought her groceries on Fridays. And so, despite her tender muscles and worn out nerves, Miss Martin drove to the store. Because she had a schedule. Because it was the responsible thing to do, and if Miss Martin was anything, she was responsible.

She didn't bring a list—didn't need one. She bought the same items every week: milk—always skim, cat food, bananas—high in potassium, other sundries, but never more than she could carry out on her own.

Miss Martin pushed her cart to the return by the store's entrance and as she went to pick up her bags, she heard a man's voice behind her. "Lisa?"

She'd been Miss Martin for so long, even to her colleagues, that she didn't recognize it as her own name.

"Lisa Martin?"

She turned, and there he was. David Jameson. She hadn't seen him since the day she had ended things with him. How difficult it had been to break up with a man she still loved. Even now, more than twenty years later, it pinched deep inside.

Within an hour of telling him it was over, she'd longed to take it back, but that was the weakness of the heart; it wasn't rational. It hadn't been a decision she'd made lightly, either. It was through lots of thought she had determined that they just weren't right for each other, didn't make any sense for them to be together. So, she had said goodbye. It was the responsible thing to do. She cut her phone cord, so she couldn't call him. Endured sleepless nights. And when, after several months with no appetite, she still found her days and nights consumed with thoughts of David Jameson, she picked a date to let him go. And after that day, if thoughts of David came to her, and they often did, then she'd find things to keep her busy. Miss Martin, who was a student then, volunteered for extra projects, took up running, studied Spanish. And she was very, very busy.

It was the right choice, though. One glance told her that. Dickies pants, hard-toed shoes, a button up shirt with "Dave" embroidered in red floss on an oval patch. The darkness around his fingernails and settled into the lines of his knuckles. The tang of grease or oil. She remembered the waxy feel of his hands, even after they were washed.

His hairline had receded, there were streaks of gray in his side-burns and wrinkles around his eyes. But, no, he hadn't changed. Probably working in the same garage, and hanging out with the same old friends.

In college, she'd read Plato, Aristotle, Nietzsche—and their words expanded in her mind. She'd walk in circles around her apartment, deep in thought, wondering what reality really is, where morals come from, the impact of society on behaviors. Sometimes she'd speak aloud, gesturing with her hands.

"Who cares?" David had said one day.

She'd forgotten he was there. Looked and found him slouched on her couch. He raised a can to her. "A beer, a game, and life is good."

"Really?" she asked. "That's all?"

He looked at her blankly, blinked a couple times, then smiled goofily. "Well, and you, Babe."

Yes, she'd been right to end things. Better to be alone than to be with the wrong man, and if David Jameson was anything, he was the wrong man.

"It's been a long time," David said.

"Yes, it has," said Miss Martin. "What have you been up to?"

"Oh, you know. Same ol', same ol'. You married now?"

She shook her head.

"Yeah, me neither."

He helped carry some of her bags and walked her to her car. She opened her trunk; they put the bags inside.

"Gosh, it's good to see you." David said. "Hey, you know what we should do? We should go to that café on Center, get some coffee. Catch up a little."

Miss Martin knew it was time to say goodbye again. This time for good. She closed the trunk. "Look, I—" she began.

A sudden gust blew between them. The gale chased around Miss Martin like a whirlwind. Undid her bun, flared her skirt. Breathed into her skin. It danced around her, singing a secret song.

When the wind finally eased, Lisa stepped back. Her hair loosed, eyes glistening, her blood now injected with new energy; she laughed.

And David laughed. "You were saying?" he asked.

She tucked her hair behind her ear. The wind had moved elsewhere, but she could still hear it whispering the word it'd stolen from her. "Look, look, look."

And Lisa looked at David with her windswept eyes and said, "I'd love to, Dave."

DESERT MUSTANG

Jeffery Bateman

To run is to live, sage slaps at his knees,
alone with the kiss of a warm, desert breeze.

Alert in the silent, desolate space,
untouched by man, a state of grace.

Competing for fodder, water and space,
too many horses for this harsh place.

Hammering, chopping the dry desert air;
it swoops down low, driving them—where?

Instinct against them, they move as one,
white-eyed panic, onward they run.

Corralled, crowded, they strike out in fear,
surrounded by steel, freedom so near.

Flat hand to muzzle, a tentative touch,
a start towards trust, it means so much.

Skin quivering under the path of my hand,
afraid but not bolting, now part of our band.

Halters and lead ropes, lariats, spurs,
patient progression, steady nerves.

First saddle, first bridle, first weight on his back,
no bucking, no kicking with each piece of tack.

Hundred-day champion, put to the test,
he proved his mettle, became the best.

Friend and companion, trust built two ways,
alone but together the rest of our days.

LOOKING FOR LINES

Felicia Rose

Few lessons I learned in Orthodox Jewish Girls' School remain as clear as that of looking for lines. We girls applied ourselves to this skill with the same devotion the boys of our tribe studied Scripture. Take for instance the day Miriam Baila's mother came to our sixth grade class to give a lesson on knitting.

"Cast on," she said. "Good. Now, knit. Purl. Knit. Purl. Wrap the yarn over the needle. Good. Now, under the needle. Knit. Purl. Keep going. Very good."

A petite woman with serious eyes and shoulder-length hair, she stood by the chalkboard, knitting needles in hand, a skein of yarn on the desk. We sat in two long rows following her lead with our own knitting needles and yarn, all of us wearing the same navy skirts, which covered our knees, and the same long-sleeved blouses buttoned to the collar.

"Knit. Purl." she continued. "Good. Now, cast off."

At recess, Batya and I stood by the synagogue, which doubled as our school. A lady resembling Miriam Baila's mother walked by, four young children in tow. *Lashon ha-ra*—the sin of gossip—ignored, Batya asked if I thought Miriam Baila's mother wore a wig. "Her hairline seems real," she said. She adjusted the headband on her own wavy blonde hair. "She's probably one of those shameless women who goes around showing her hair."

"Maybe it's a really expensive wig," I said. "With those it's hard to tell."

"I doubt it. And besides, her stockings don't have lines," she added, referring to the custom among many Orthodox women of wearing stockings with seams along the back of the leg.

❧

Like well-trained spies, we girls remained alert to the secret codes of our tribe, and to the slightest infractions. Not even teachers escaped scrutiny. Mrs. Stern, for instance, wore a stiff brown wig. On one occasion it slipped exposing brunette hair beneath. Mrs. Zucker, the Rabbi's wife, shaved her head. This became apparent when *her* wig slipped, and her hairline revealed a mere shadow of reddish-brown stubble. When Miss Roth became Mrs. Katz, she covered her long blonde hair with a long blonde wig. Such details informed the gossip-filled notes we exchanged as one teacher or the other stood at the chalkboard parsing a line from Leviticus or praising the modesty of the Biblical Ruth.

The Ruth in our class did not always pass muster in that regard. Tall and lean, she grew even taller and leaner during a growth spurt in the seventh grade. "Take this note to the Rabbi's office where you will wait until your mother comes with a suitable skirt," Mrs. Rimler said. Her own hemline modestly grazed her ankles.

Standing in line outside school that morning, I could have predicted it. "Look at Ruthie's skirt," I'd whispered to Batya. "You can practically see her knees."

"It's shameful, really. Don't her parents love her?"

Having spent several Sabbaths at Ruthie's home, I imagined they did. I also knew they were tired and poor, and that Ruthie was the youngest of nine. And though they took pains to send all nine children to religious school and to live a devout life, monitoring Ruthie's hemline may have been more than they could abide.

❧

In nearly all aspects of life, lines mattered. The line between Sabbath and work week, dairy and meat, gentile and Jew. To cross lines, or even to blur them, constituted blasphemy. Even the lower-case 't' needed to be written with a right-facing hook at the bottom lest it resemble a cross. We girls imbibed our lessons well. Out of fear of God or parents or teachers or the perennial gossip of classmates, we wrote our 't's to resemble umbrella handles. Certain no other religion cared about such matters, we knew these pieties constituted yet another line separating them from us.

JUST SO

Marilyn Richardson

Serene Doreen seems to preen as she sits just so, composing her face, her smile, her hair, the vacant look in her eyes, a surprise. Can someone so pretty be empty? Does she want? Does she sigh, as she sits just so, politely, brightly, with control? Does she say with her eyes and her tight smile and the just so tilt of her head, don't probe, don't question, I'm here, that's enough.

A rebuff? I'm unsure so I ask, "What's inside, are you strong, were you wronged, do you long for attention and time? Do you find life a bore? What's more, do you think or just shrink from all conflict and woe, smiling out at the world without warmth?"

Oh, so you just want to know, says Doreen, serene, in the silent cocoon of her room.

You'd better watch out or I might tell all of the sin and the pain that is mine.

I sit, just so, with meaning unclear because of what has gone on. I could shock you, I know, with my tale of woe, of incest, of death and decay. Between grin and grim lies the subtle lilt of my lips held so. I look out, hold in, hold all, to keep from scratching out my eyes, slamming my head to the wall, screaming on and on without end.

Serene Doreen, eyes dead and defeated looks out, look in, with denial. Best let her lament as she sits, just so, composing her face, her smile, her hair. I shrink from her pain with nothing to say as I leave her there with her vacant stare, alone.

THE KID

Tim Keller

The first time Jack saw the kid, Marcus Sedberry disappeared forever. That's when it started. It was also the last time Jack and his friends would be free of watchful eyes and dire admonition whenever they so much as twitched.

"Remember what happened to little Marcus," mothers would tell their children.

Jack remembered.

❦

"Now you stay close, Jackson Harris," Mama said, tying his hood under his chin. "There's some candy in your pocket for a snack, and don't go so far I can't see you."

"Yes Mama, I know," he said, already racing for the swings. Jack loved to see how high he could go. If he closed his eyes, it felt like flying, not that he'd ever tell her that. *Someday, I'll swing so high, I'll go all the way around the top bar. Then I'll tell her. Maybe.*

Someday for sure, but today Jack's cheeks were getting cold. It hadn't snowed yet, but, "the weather guy said it might," Mama said. He hated when she was right. It was too cold to swing, so he climbed the steps up the slide, and huddled in the enclosure at the top.

He looked around the yard. All the leaves were off the trees and the grass was yellowy-brown. At the end of the cul-de-sac were the woods, naked and dead looking. Across the street, Marcus kicked aimlessly around the driveway on his bike.

Jack didn't think Marcus was so little. *Marcus is a chub*, that's what Mama said to call it. "Fat is mean," she'd said. "Say chubby instead."

Marcus saw him and called, "Hey, wanna come over? I got a new bike."

Jack hesitated. "Fat" might be mean, but Marcus could be too, and he was two years older, though only a grade ahead.

Mama's probably asleep, he thought. Which meant he had until his father got home, *at least an hour*, and Marcus's house was "close."

"Come on," Marcus called. "Don't you wanna see?"

Jack cast a look back at his house, then jogged over. "Sure is a great bike," he offered, tracing the fire-engine red and orange flames with his finger.

"Yup, and it's real fast; nobody but me can ride it. You can watch though."

Jack shrugged. It wasn't exactly his idea of a good time, but neither was sitting alone in the cold.

"Marcus?" his mother called from the doorway. "Who's out there with you?"

"It's only Jacky Ma, geez."

"Oh, hello Jacky," she said, rubbing her arms. "What are you boys doing out in the cold?"

"I just want to show him how I can ride my new bike," Marcus said.

"Well, all right, but be back in an hour for supper."

Marcus threw a *chubby* leg over the seat, sort of hauling himself on. "Watch this!" He puffed, weaving drunkenly down the street toward the woods. Jack followed half-jogging, half-walking with his hands shoved in his pocket, as the bike wobbled from curb to curb. Even in the cold, the swing set at home began to look pretty good.

A passing car honked and made Marcus swerve. The bike slipped out from under him, throwing him onto the sidewalk.

"Oow!" he cried, rubbing a hamburger sized scrape on his arm.

That's when the kid showed up. He was about Jack's age, maybe a little older.

Marcus looked up at him.

"Great bike," the kid said. "Can I ride it?"

Marcus stopped crying and stood up. "No!" he shouted. "Nobody's supposed to but me."

I wanna see him ride, Jack thought.

The kid winked at him. Jack remembered that—the wink. Later, when he was asked to recall all he could, he couldn't remember much, just the wink, that and the eyes. The kid had big round eyes, like Jack's, and he liked the way they looked.

"I'll trade you this," the kid said, holding out a Babe Ruth. Marcus snatched the bar and headed toward the woods, the kid in tow.

"Hey! wait up," Jack said.

"Go home little baby!" Marcus called back to him.

Jack didn't say that part though; that would have been telling, and telling was "mean."

Later, at the police station, while his father and a policeman talked, Jack asked, "Do you think they threw Marcus's supper away?"

"Hush!" his mother said.

"They went in the woods," Jack told the policeman. The kid pushed the bike while Marcus ate.

"That's all you remember? You're sure?"

"Yup"

"And you're sure what you told Officer Thomas here was true?" Jack's father asked. "You didn't make any of it up?"

"Joe," his mother whispered—"Jacky wouldn't make up something like this."

A single look silenced her, *the mean look.*

Jack shook his head.

"Jackson, this is very important," Officer Thomas said. "If you saw that boy again, the one who gave Marcus the candy, would recognize him?"

Jack nodded.

❧

The next time he saw the kid, Jack was holding the ladder while his father fixed the antenna on the roof.

Jack recognized him by his eyes, as he sat across the street watching them.

"Dad" Jack called up to his father.

"Don't come up here Jacky, it's dangerous."

"But dad, it's the kid I saw with Marcus!" he whisper-shouted.

"Who?"

The ladder lurched.

"Damnit Jackson! I told you to hold the ladder, not daydream.

"You never listen!" Jack yelled. "It's the kid who killed Marcus, Don't you see him?"

He didn't. He didn't see the leg of the ladder sliding out either. Jacky watched spellbound as his father spun into the air, and smashed with a thud against the driveway.

Brains splashed onto Jack's sneaker. "He was mean," the kid said, suddenly beside them.

"It's dangerous up there," Jack said blankly.

The kid winked.

By the time Jack's mother came shrieking out the door, the kid was gone.

REMEMBERING BRENDA

Isaac Timm

Deep creek, in the wind-blown valley
calls its bones home. The memory-dream,
blonde-haired girl who called me tiger, who disappeared,
but did not run away, did not run away over the hills
golden hair flying, did not run away at all but lay in the salt
marsh reeds until they raised her bones,
the saints that places her on linen cloth, saints that gave her
bones to her mother,

the mother that buried her daughter without a coffin,
under the painting, from the portrait, taken before
June of nineteen seventy-nine, after the spring
her grandmother brought her to my fourth birthday
after she gave me a silver foil box with a robin's egg
blue bow. And I can't remember what it was, what she
gave me, and I should remember. But the mother remembered
never forgot, even after the day she brought her daughter
back and placed her in the family plot, where the meadow
grass grows, gold in October, haloed in light the memory-dream
and a silver foil box, and the girl that will run forever
before the wind that calls her.

AURA

Dianne Hardy

I'm feline, a smuggled cat, not allowed where I live, Palatial Living in Logan, Utah. Fancy name for a trailer park, huh? My Mom got me five years ago through a newspaper ad. I came free of charge, didn't cost her one red cent. That made her happy because she's tight. In fact she rarely talks about money other than to mutter something about it being the root of all evil.

She tries to make me feel guilty when I refuse to eat dry cat food saying, "Don't be ungrateful, Aura. When I was a kid people drowned whole litters of baby cats." I think that's completely off the subject and shouldn't a writer know better? You see, as a baby I was given canned cat food once at my other house and that kind of pleasure stays with you, ya know?

☙

Within days of getting me she had me 'fixed.' Ridiculous because being contraband I'm housebound, never been outdoors. I only learned about that sex stuff last summer when she held me up to the window where we watched a couple of cats in the grip of ecstasy. At first it looked interesting; the big orange-striped one clamping down on the black one's head—had her right between his jaws. Just envisioning a fight made my hair stand on end. I was a howling as loud as they were, but safe on my side. Then the mean one quit biting and I think, went to sleep on the other one's back. Much ado about nothing, so I made my way to the computer monitor for a nap. Mom got a real kick out of it, stayed watching until the big one left.

☙

Sleeping's my life. Mom claims I do too much, but she's just jealous because she

can't sleep through a night. Needing to pee gets her up and Facebook keeps her up. At three in the morning for God's sake!

She buys stupid toys to intrigue me, like I've forgotten how to play or something. One worked for a short time. A red dot circling the room had me running helter-skelter; until I realized she was controlling the event. That's when I ignored it and between you and me, that was hard as hell.

☙

I'm not your ordinary run-of-the-mill cat. Mom's not ordinary either. We're both gifted…you know, psychically. She says she checked out cats before me and none of them spoke to her soul.

According to her I was crying inconsolably. The kid who was giving me and my siblings away actually tried to dissuade her from choosing me. Pointing he said, "That one is the smallest, the least ready to wean. She's the runt of the litter."

Mom paid him no attention, simply went with her intuition as usual. As I settled down, nestling comfortably in the palm of her hand, we bonded. On the way home she proclaimed:

I need you, tiny girl.
You smoky ball of fluff
with eyes of karmic bent
to atone my deficit.
You'll be my Aura.

☙

95

Life hasn't all been rosy. Cats are supposed to be independent. Although embarrassed to admit it, I'm downright needy at times. It's Mom's fault because she's pre-occupied with her music, spending hours at the piano, oblivious to me.

Getting her attention is easier when she talks on the phone and I bite her foot—not hard, just enough to irritate her. She'll yell, "You little shit," and toss me across the room. I just haven't found anything to work where music is involved.

Wikipedia says "If you can't beat them join them" means admitting defeat and showing a willingness to work with 'them.' That's what I decided to do with Mom.

I started listening to the music she plays. Much of it is popular stuff from the 1950s—her day, but some is high-brow and technical like the music of Beethoven. To my surprise, I found I rather like him.

So when she plays the *Moonlight Sonata,* I come running and sing along. Moonlight does that to me, fence or no fence. *Für Elise* makes me content enough to fall asleep in the middle. Mom doesn't notice whether I'm singing or sleeping because, like I said, at the piano she's in her own world.

That Beethoven must have been one talented guy. He wrote beautiful music when he was deaf—by just hearing it in his head. He sounds rather psychic to me; I think maybe he's one of 'us.'

ဆ

Besides music, Mom's fanatic about books; they're all over the place, even on our bed. I have to say their attraction escapes me. While okay to lie on, they're not like a box you can climb into and hide. Plus, the content! The stuff she reads can give an ordinary person nightmares—stories by Flannery O'Conner or Stephen King. I've decided all authors are disturbed.

ဆ

On weekends we get company, Mom's kids—Toni, Rachel, and Glen. They treat me like an interloper, rather than a sister, especially Glen, who makes fun of me. I don't know why, I've never done a thing to him. And the grandkids are the worst, hissing back at me, making faces, pointing, and trying to get at my belly. In defense I once bit one and got shut away in the bedroom. I was punished…not him.

In spite of our trials me and Mom have gotten closer over time. You can tell it by simply looking at me, fat and contented, like her, I guess. I used to sleep curled up in a ball, but now I lie stretched out flat, even on my back. She laughs and once said, "You're letting it all hang out, huh Aura?"

As I said, she's psychic like me. She knows when the phone's going to ring and who will be calling. Once she ran to comb her hair and put on lipstick, nearly stepped on me. When I yelled in protest, she said, "Get out of my way, company's coming," and sure enough Ted, our writer friend, showed up a minute later. He always says 'hi' to me before he does her—I love him.

༒

Last summer I had a horrendous encounter with a yellow cat. I sat watching a robin out front when this big guy jumped up on our porch. Viciously, we fought through the screen until Mom, hearing the ruckus, chased the ugly one away. I fled under our bed and stayed for hours. Sheesh, I wondered if my tail would ever go back to normal.

༒

Mom often sings to me while we're in our cushy, blue chair. It's the place in the house where I have her completely to myself. That's because she and I are the only ones that ever sit in it. Long ago Glen gave the chair a bad rap due to my gray hair pasted here and there.

When he says, "Mom, that chair's loaded with cat hair—you need to vacuum it," she obeys, but his efforts to make me look bad don't work. She and I appreciate the blending of blue and gray because we're sensitive to creative expression—art—which he doesn't understand being obsessive compulsive, plus an intolerant redneck.

Anyway, Mom owns hundreds of CDs. My all-time favorite is one of Jim Reeves. We were sitting in our chair listening one day. I was dozing in and out, lulled by the opening strains of "Four Walls."

Jim's caressing voice began: "Out where the bright lights are glowing, you're drawn like a moth to a flame..." I shot up, wide awake. A moth? Where? I'd like to get my paws on that.

☙

Last year a major crisis fastened me and Mom together as tight as glue. I've always known when she was going to leave me—even before she hauled out the suitcase. I'd tried lying on top of it in protest. I'd also hidden, refusing to say good-bye, but neither ever kept her home. She'd only stay away for a short time, a couple of days at the most.

Last September when she left it felt different. Instead of driving her car she went away with Glen... and stayed away. Every few days he'd let himself into our house and call, "Where's my good kitty?" like Mom does. The first time it happened I fell for it and came running—but never again.

Hiding under the bed I thought, *fool me once, shame on you; fool me twice, shame on me.* You know I'm pretty smart; I said that better than that one guy—who was he? Oh yeah, Former President George Bush! He was before my time, but Mom must have liked him because she's always imitating him in a funny voice and finishing with 'heh, heh.'

While at our house when Mom was gone, Glen would set out food and fresh water. Then he'd start shoveling shit out of my litter box. Within a minute he'd be gagging and cussing like a preacher. Ah, sweet revenge.

☙

Well, the separation wore on both me and Mom. When she came home three weeks later I was hoarse from crying and wild with fear, not about to let her touch me. Come to think of it, she didn't even try.

She looked scary, had to use a walker just to go from our chair to the bathroom, and she winced with every step. Worst yet, she stared straight ahead all day, no writing, playing the piano—nothing. When the telephone rang she didn't answer, and Glen had to use his key to get in the house because she wouldn't go to the door.

98

He'd come in, heat up a can of chicken noodle soup and sit and watch her eat it. That's when I knew for certain something was wrong, because she used to eat all the time, even in the night, and now she didn't want to.

After a week Glen was tired of it, pissed off royally in fact. "Goddammit Mom, you're going to promise me you won't do anything bad or you have to go live with Rachel so she can watch you. Now which will it be?"

When Mom didn't answer, he yelled, "Either way your cat will be gone because none of us kids can take her. We already have animals, and she won't be able to adapt. You're all she's got."

Mom looked over at me, seemed to really notice me for the first time in a long time. I quit licking myself and watched her back. After what felt like an eternity she softly said, "I promise, Glen. I won't do anything bad," and broke down crying.

He softened. "I know it's hard. Losing music must feel like death to you, but the doctors say when the drugs are finally out of your system you might be able to play again. We've got to be patient."

☙

All three kids were at our house the following week.

"Well Mom, you're looking better than you did when you first had the knee replacement," Toni said. "Sorry, I couldn't stay longer. When I left Roosevelt it was quiet and then just when you came out of surgery, I got a call from my boss saying we had three to embalm. That's the life of a mortician—I'm always on call whether it's slow or they're dying like flies."

I like that. Once I found one, a fly on the window sill—killed and ate it, slicker than shit!

"When did you notice Mom wasn't all right?" Toni asked.

"She was doing well but in a lot of pain while still in the hospital, so they gave her more drugs," Glen said.

"Yeah," Rachel agreed. "Two days later they took her to the Sunshine Terrace to recover. She was on massive doses of morphine, Valium, and Loritab, all at the same time. We were in her room visiting when someone turned on the TV. It was LDS conference

99

and Mom blurted out, "Turn that off. It's a conspiracy."

Toni laughed. "I've never once heard her use that word."

"We hadn't either," Glen agreed.

"I still feel bad for the help," said Rachel. "The lady on night shift was sweet and caring, but the more patient she was the worse Mom treated her—called her Nurse Ratchett in Pink."

"Oh, that's terrible," Toni cried, "Do you think she got it?"

Mom stared straight ahead, but I got it; I'm not called Aura for nothing! I looked over at *One Flew Over the Cuckoo's Nest* sitting on the bookcase shelf. Mom loves Jack Nicholson because they're both rebels.

"The nurse was probably too young to know the movie," Rachel said. "At any rate, the place got its fill of Mom, said they couldn't deal with her mental condition if it continued. They told us to start looking into lockdown places, didn't they Glen?"

"Yep. After a couple of days the doctor reduced her medication; still she was 'out of it' for a while. The worst was day four when she met her physical therapist there at the rehab place. An attendant told her to wait in a large room where there were no chairs. I think he thought she'd use her wheel chair. But Mom went with her walker and finding no chairs, she sat down on the piano bench.

The therapist came in, introduced himself and seeing her at the piano said, "Do you play, Dianne?"

"Yes, she said, placing her hands on the keys. Glen paused. "Evidently she couldn't play a note, and she's been suicidal at different times since. The doctor advised us not to push the music playing. He said Mom would know when the time was right to try. It hasn't happened yet."

ɛ⌃ɔ

So that's it! Here I was thinking the problem was her knee. I should have known it was caused by music and that's why I'd catch her staring at the piano. It also explains the day she hugged me hard enough I had trouble breathing. She cried, "Aura, Aura, help me. Music's been with me longer than anything in my life." All I could do was lick her, but I did that until my tongue was sore.

I guess I should be grateful to the kids for finally getting answers. Nobody tells a cat anything. Over time Mom began to walk better and her appetite came back. When I heard her humming "Stayin' Alive," I knew we'd make it. Still, I watched her closely, lay on her lap purring—whole days sometimes.

☙

Her thirteenth day home, I awoke to find her shuffling through movies. She reached for *The Hours*. Knowing I'd better do something drastic, I leapt onto the chair, flew over to the shelf, and knocked *Awakenings* to the floor. It's about patients in a hospital for the chronically ill and a doctor who brings them out of a catatonic state.

"Dammit all, Aura. Look what you've done," she yelled, shoving me to the floor. But she picked up the box, thought a moment, and put the movie into the machine. There's a scene where the doctor, Robin Williams, races onto the patient's ward in the middle of the night to find everyone chattering about their lives as though it were forty years before. A man sits at the grand piano playing a Cole Porter song.

Mom stared wide-eyed at the TV. Her mouth dropped open. She grabbed the remote and paused the movie. Tossing me from her lap, she rose from our chair, and hobbled to the piano.

"I can do that," she declared. Then she sat and played "The Way We Were," as though there'd been no hiatus—laughing and crying at the same time. We didn't even finish the movie.

☙

That was a year ago. Now Glen is having his own crisis. Mom has him come to eat lunch every day because he's depressed and gaunt looking. I heard her demand that he promise the same thing she promised him, not to do anything bad.

I'm actually getting more used to him. Instead of running to hide when he comes, I stay put on our chair. Mom noticed and told me, "That's good, Aura. You need to be in here with us because we're a family. Maybe you can help him like you did me."

I think tragedy makes people change because yesterday he petted me.

We'll see.

RACCOON SHUFFLE

Marie Tollstrup

In darkness or by lanterned-moon,
I await his nocturnal audition
when he does the raccoon shuffle,
eluding me in my backyard.
He dances in obsidian shadows,
an evasive, masked intruder.

Day rips away his cover
as he escapes to his rock cave lair.
I know he's invaded again
by his handiwork. His fancy footwork
reveals a lawn in tatters, sod overturned,
annoying as moth holes in my prized sweater.

He must know I'm a woman
because he eludes me each night.
I feel stood up, waiting for his invitation
to do the raccoon shuffle as a couple.

I change strategies. A trap waits.
Now I entice him with hotdog bits.
True, not as succulent as his juicy grubs.
My goal—to capture him once and for all.
At daybreak I survey my lawn
and look for signs of the raccoon shuffle.
My eyes downcast, I near the trap.
Voila! I behold his theatrical eyes.

Victory swells within—
my hunt now a notch on my belt.
He slinks lower in the trap,
eyeing me warily, imploring me.
I've got you, my lovely, a worthy opponent.
You will be relocated to woodland wilds
my sweet, where you can dance
the raccoon shuffle from dark to dawn.

MIRRORED REALITIES

Sherrie Lynn Clarke

"Sometimes, I wish a bus would ram into my car."

Dr. #7's head jerked up from her paperwork. "What?"

"It's nothing."

"Do you feel that often?" she asked, her voice measured.

My eyes shifted to the window. Lavender scented air freshener filled the room to tease my inconsolable heart.

"Have you been taking your medication?"

"Yes."

"Are you lying?"

I gazed back at Dr. #7's formal eyes. "No. I take a pill every day."

"Does it stop those desires?"

I twisted my ring around and around my finger. "Yes."

"If it doesn't, I can change your prescription."

"It's helping."

When I got home I took two pills; the silence cuddled me as I lay down and slept.

☙

Laughter dances around me in the mist.

☙

The Awakening fell into my lap as I stared out the bay window. I sat on the sill, which had been fashioned as a bench. Autumn chill seeped through the glass while stagnant air parched my mouth. The pressure of silence numbed my ears, mocking my soul where the laugh of a little girl once resonated. My eyes pinched shut while the conflicting senses raged a battle, hollowing out my chest. I entered the kitchen, grabbed a bottle, and jiggled four pills into my hand. While I walked back to the window, I threw them into my mouth and read *The Awakening* until I fell asleep.

ᘒ

Samantha runs, pressing her toes into the grass. I follow.
"Here, Momma!"
The blanket flies out for the picnic pie.

ᘒ

In her room, I looked through the clothes. I held each tiny pink item up for a moment and laid them down in a line.
"What are you doing?"
"I didn't know you were home," I said. Dust tickled my nose.
John rested his hand on my shoulder. "What are you doing?"
"Remembering." I set the seventh piece on the ground.
"Are you stable enough for this?" His voice chapped my ears.
I didn't answer.
"Have you taken your pill today?"
I stood and turned away, headed to the kitchen. "Maybe not."

ᘒ

Samantha holds my hand before she runs to show me a blue rose. It sparkles in the sun.
"Lookie, Momma!"
I look close; there are no thorns. Perfect.
"It smells good."
She inhales. "Yeah, like strawberries!"

ᘒ

My head lay against the back of the rocker; John spoke with Dr. #7 on the kitchen phone.

"I'm concerned about her," he whispered.

I stood and entered the kitchen; picked up the bottle. Six pills.

He saw me. "Haven't you already had one?" His rough face matched his voice.

My head shook. "Not today."

ℭ

At the top of a steep slope, a tree grew almost horizontal.

"Momma, watch me!"

Samantha walks across it and sits down. Allowing her feet to dangle, she waves them sporadically back and forth.

"Come sit!" she calls, giggling.

I sit, and we pretend to swing, hand in hand. The smell of leaves surrounds us.

ℭ

Seven pills slid down my throat; I lay down. The absence of feeling would surround and caress me until John came home. But John was just a dream. Until I woke up, I wouldn't see Samantha.

ℭ

Her hair shines in the sun, a radiant red that I envy. It looks brown indoors; I love the outside more. The wind spreads around the sound of birds chirping about the birth of spring.

"Momma, I found a ladybug!" Her voice urges me to respond.

"How old is it?"

"Huh?"

"How many dots does it have?"

"Um..." Her head turns to the side; I smile. "I can't tell! It keeps moving!"

"That's because it would have to grant you a wish if you knew."

"Really?" She chases it saying, "Buggie! Wish!"

ℭ

Someone rubbed my cheek, a soft caress that I knew.

"Please wake up, honey."

I would wake up. With Samantha.

ⲥⲟ

"What would you have wished for, if you could have counted the dots?" I ask.

"Easy!" She snuggles up next to me. "I want to do this all the time–every day!"

I smile. "A picnic every day?"

"Yup!" She nods her head; her curls bounce.

I put my arm around her. "That would be nice."

I fall backward and pull her with me. She giggles as we go down, lays her head on my breast, and quickly falls asleep. The smell of grass fills my nose, and my eyes close. Something tugs my chest, threatening to tear me away. Our breaths synchronize as I rest.

ⲥⲟ

"Oh God, no!" John wailed. "Save her!"

ⲥⲟ

I feel free. Samantha's laughs swirl around me as she runs and finds more interesting things in the grass. The sun is warm, but not so warm that I feel the burn. I raise my hands slowly into the air. The outside smell of life spirals into my lungs, scattering its vitality with every beat of my heart.

"Dance with me, Momma!" Samantha calls.

I twirl around and around with the breeze; the world spins, but I don't get dizzy. The grass tickles my feet as I go faster. Samantha's laugh continues, causes me to smile, as my mouth opens and rippling tones escape into the air and dance with us.

A phantom tear brushes my cheek.

UNSTRUNG BY THE SEA

Steve Proskauer

Long sea-soaked afternoon
Thoughts washed away
Drifting
Windblown
Waves rise and fall
Gentling me

GOING SLACK

Steve Proskauer

Going slack like springs uncoiling
I nod and soften in my chair
Open book slides to the floor
Lucent strands of dream unfurl

Wafting up in misty wisps
Touching topmost twigs and needles
I float across the sheltered shallows
Fog caressing lapping ripples

Spreading, spreading
Wings of light
I glide away
Across the bay

BROKEN PELICAN

Steve Proskauer

He struggles in foam
Tumbled by waves
One wing droops
Dragging him under
Like an anchor
Drowning the diver

When you can't fly
Or even stagger
There's no safety
Even in Eden

Human help meets
Snapping beak
Guarding
Sacred death

Clutching bill
Man prevails
A fallible angel
Bearing the bird
Up and away
To purgatory

THE BURDEN OF FORGETTING

Amanda Luzzader

Inside the small cottage, Connor's belongings cluttered tables, overflowed from bookcases, and even lined the flooring, pushed to the edges of the walls.

Connor sat cross-legged on the floor, flipping through the pages of a worn book.

"What are you looking for?" asked little Anya.

"The same thing I'm always looking for," Connor replied.

"But, Uncle," she fiddled with her blonde braid, "ye've never told me what 'tis."

"I'll know once I find it."

His possessions had piled up over the years like sediment. Mostly they were things he'd collected during his travels. There was a jar of turquoise mermaid scales, gifted to him by a clan of the sea creatures in the Caribbean. An envelope containing golden Pegasus feathers, collected from the ground after a failed attempt at riding the beautiful creature. A clay pot of poppy dust, carefully gathered from the fields of Avalon. And of course, Connor had his books, enough to fill a library even without counting the thick, leather-bound journals in which he'd diagramed the flora and fauna of all the places he'd visited. But now, instead of being a happy reminder of the good life he had lived, the items felt like a build-up of plaque in his arteries; they only burdened his heart.

There were days when Connor's empty searches overwhelmed him so much that he'd stay in bed for days with no motivation to get up, not even to eat. But inevitably, sweet Anya, wearing her white frock, would appear by his bedside. She brought bread or soup from her mama. Sometimes she'd bring flowers and tuck one behind his ear. But even on the days when she came empty-handed, somehow the presence of the cheery, blue-eyed girl gave Connor the courage he needed to get up and search once more.

"What's this now?" Anya asked, plucking something from a trunk.

Connor looked up from the canister he was searching. "Dragon's toenail."

Each time he answered one question, an onslaught of more questions followed.

"How did ye get it? Where did it come from? Weren't ye scared the dragon would wake up and bite off yer head?"

When Anya tired of searching, she climbed into the wide frame of Connor's window. Light streamed through the bubbled glass, illuminating her face as she hummed random notes that didn't belong to any particular song, but somehow formed their own tune.

Abruptly, she stopped humming.

"I've decided something."

"What's that, wee one?" Connor asked while standing knee deep in a pile of papers.

"I'm going to be an adventurer just like you."

He turned so she wouldn't see the joyful tears brimming in his eyes.

"You'll have to grow a wee bit first."

"How much?"

"At least high e'nuff to reach the branches of the apple tree."

"Why'd ye quit your travelin'?"

Connor thought about telling Anya how all the treasures he had collected over his lifetime amounted to next to nothing compared to the days he spent with her and her family. Instead, he sniffed and said, "Me knees wore out."

At last the sun began slinking behind the green hills. Connor closed the box he had just searched.

"Well, me lass, let's call it a day. Yonder tavern's calling me name." He hobbled to the door. "C'mere and give ye Uncle a hug before ye go off now."

Standing on her tip-toes, she kissed his cheek, as she always did, and said, "Love ye, Uncle. I hope ye find what ye are looking for."

❧

The Purple Heather tavern sat in the hollow of two hills. The patrons were mostly merchants and farmers—friends who had grown up together. Once or twice a year, a new face would appear—a traveler passing through—and the regulars could never pass by sharing their stories to fresh ears. The visitor this day was a tall, pale man, and he sat at a full table.

Jess McCourt wrapped his thick and hairy arm around the shoulder of his new friend. Ale sloshed from his mug, and the tavern's dry oak table drank up the spills.

"Here right now we are in the company of the luckiest man alive," McCourt told the stranger. He pointed to a younger, brawny man with curly hair and ruddy cheeks. "That's the one right there."

Before the visitor could reply, McCourt added, "And we've the unluckiest man as well." He pointed again to the same man. "And there he be."

The men laughed.

"Now, ye may be wonderin' how that 'tis."

The traveler nodded.

"Tomas here was given a fairy wish at birth. Good for anything in the whole world," McCourt said. "That makes him the luckiest man alive, ya see. But, 'twas his uncle that gave it to him with the condition that he gets the say-so on any wish."

"Aye!" Shane O'Brennan shouted. "And the old stodge always says 'No!'"

McCourt frowned at O'Brennan. "Right. So, that makes Tomas the unluckiest, too."

"I'd start by wishing for a new uncle," someone yelled out, and no one laughed harder than the wrinkled man in the corner, the uncle in question, Connor McBride.

Tomas walked over to his uncle and put his hand on his shoulder.

"Friends," he said, "let me assure you, I am indeed the luckiest man. First, for having such a generous uncle. Second, for owning an unwished wish, and lastly, because me uncle is so wise. I've begged since I was a boy to use me wish on everything from candy to toys, but Uncle knew better."

"There's no wish," Keevan Peters said. "The old man's playing ye fer a fool."

"On the grave of me dear mother, I swear 'tis true." Connor raised his cane in his long, bony hand and shook it. He struggled to stand. The crowd quieted as Connor relayed the tale he'd told them so many times before. "I'd just received news of Tomas's birth. Me first nephew. So, I was rushing home to see the lad. And as I was running through the forest, I happened to come upon this fox. Seeing my ol' mug startled him to the point that he fled through the heather, but he first dropped something from his mouth. Looked like a wad of leaves."

Connor's eyes glowed. "Now why would a fox be interested in some old leaves? I knelt down and saw t'wasn't leaves at all, but the ugliest fairy I ever had the misfortune of laying me eyes upon. A furry brown moth with a teeny-tiny human attached. I picked her up into me hands; she was all wet and mangled. I was going to take her home, I was, for me collections, but I saw the smallest flutter of life. So, I cupped me hands around her and blew slowly over the wee thing. Ever so slowly her glow returned, and I come to find out that I had saved none other than the fairy queen, herself. She offered me the world. I only asked for one thing in return. A gift for me new nephew." Connor pounded his cane on the ground to punctuate his last words, "The lad has a wish."

"Don't doubt it," O'Brennan said, "Connor McBride's an honest man."

"Hear, hear!" the men shouted.

"I once asked for riches," Tomas said. "Uncle said, 'No.' What did I get instead? A strong back working in the fields, pride from doing me own labor, and enough coins to pay me debts with a little left over for drinks with me friends. Enough to make me happy. When

I fancied Kelly Allen and she wouldn't look twice at me, I asked Uncle to make her look again. He refused and instead I found me eternal love, me darling Clara. If I lack for anything, it is only the knowledge of what to wish for. My dear uncle is too wise to let me waste me wish."

"Ay, the boy just doesn't know what he wants!" Connor stood, leaning on his cane because of his rounded back. He squeezed Tomas's arm.

The other patrons began bombarding Tomas with wish ideas—a new dray horse, conversation with the dead, a bottomless ale mug.

As their conversation grew louder, Connor snuck out the side door and hurried home.

The talk at the tavern had constricted his throat and caused his stomach to ache. He lit a candle and limped over to two piles of books stacked in the corner. One pile he had searched already; in the other pile were books he needed to check, but he did not remember which was which. He sighed and toppled the towers into each other. In the flickering light of the candle, Connor sat in the muddle, picked up a book, and examined its pages, starting with the cover. He'd been searching now for ten long years.

It was true that Connor had waited for Tomas to be old enough to understand what he was wishing for, but he had decided that Tomas would be ready after his twentieth birthday. Shortly after the date passed, Connor spotted Tomas walking up his path and could tell from his nephew's gait that the young man had a wish in mind. He hurried to the door and danced a little jig, despite his achy joints. Then he swung the door open and ushered Tomas inside.

"I'd like to use me wish," Tomas said. "I want a large house with a big fruitful garden."

"A big one, eh?" Connor smiled, and his heart pounded in anticipation.

"That's right," Tomas said. "A place to call me own."

Connor nodded and opened his mouth to pronounce the wish, but suddenly discovered the words weren't there. The phrase the fairies had taught him was inexplicably absent from his memory.

"I can't grant the wish," Connor muttered, mostly to himself, but

Tomas having been denied so many times before, took his words as an injunction.

"I understand," Tomas said. He hugged his uncle and headed back to the fields.

Surely, I'd have written down something so important, Connor thought. But as days turned into years, and Connor's search through his house and books proved fruitless, he started to suspect that all those years ago, when the fairies gave him the wish, he must have thought he didn't need to write it down. *Because how could anyone forget something so important?*

Except for the occasional visit to the Purple Heather, Connor spent all his time looking for the magical words. He'd thought about confessing his memory lapse a thousand times, but each time he'd think of the townsfolk and what they'd say about him. That he was a liar. Or worse, that he was the bumbling old fool who had ruined everything for his nephew.

Still, he thought he could bear their judgment. What he knew he could not stand was Tomas's disappointment. He pictured Tomas's face, his head tilted slightly, lips pressed tight, eyes downcast—the face of someone whose whole world was stolen from them. He couldn't do that to Tomas, not to the boy he loved. So he searched through every page of every book, through every scrap of paper, examining pictures, and pottery, and statues. And all the while, he hoped if he couldn't find the words at least the search might reveal some clue to unlock the vault of his mind. The words seemed to float on the edge of his memories, ready to be recalled at any moment, yet always out of his reach.

Tomas, married and with children of his own, made a couple of wish requests each year. He'd never questioned his uncle's refusals, but Connor knew that wouldn't last forever.

The fateful day came a month after the visitor's arrival at the tavern, during the town's wet season.

The dampness made Connor's joints creak even more than usual, and the path to the Purple Heather was flooded anyway, so Connor sequestered himself at home for a week. Anya hadn't visited in few days, but Connor knew it was only because she'd been helping

Tomas in the fields.

Connor's cottage filled with warm humidity, and the scent of leather and paper fragranced the air. Thunder shook the sky in the afternoon, but as the day fell to evening, the rain turned to a gentle and steady patter that relaxed Connor as he reloaded a bookshelf of its contents.

There came a pounding at his door. He clutched the book in his hand as he turned. The door swung open, and Tomas stood dripping in the doorway. The water had taken the curl from his hair, pasting it to his forehead. His eyes were wide, and in his arms he held his youngest daughter, his little Anya.

Instead of their usual pink, her lips were an odd purple color. Her face was pale, and her eyes closed. A smear of blood matted hair to her face.

"The horses spooked," Tomas said, his voice breathy and fast.

Connor suddenly felt like the roof had torn off his house and the ice cold rain was pelting directly onto his heart. He grabbed the back of a chair to steady himself.

"My wish, Uncle." Tomas laid Anya on the table.

There was a tightness in Connor's chest; he couldn't breathe. He swallowed repeatedly.

"She's dying, Uncle." Tomas touched Connor's arm. "Make her better."

Connor walked to the table—little Anya, now so still and quiet. His chin quivered. Leaning away from the table, he turned back to Tomas.

"I can't," he whispered.

"Please, Uncle. This is all I want. This is all I'll ever want. Please, give me this wish."

"I can't do it."

In two strides, Tomas was upon him. With both hands, he lifted Connor by his shirt and dangled the old man in the air.

"Do it! Say the words!" Tomas shook him. "Give me my wish!"

"I can't, I can't." Connor sobbed. Tears streamed across his face as he shook his head. "I cannot do it."

"Uncle," Tomas's voice shook, "Please, please?"

Connor opened his mouth, but couldn't speak. He shook his head again.

Then Connor saw it: Tomas's face exactly the way he had imagined it so many times, and yet somehow a million times worse. Tomas released Connor and stepped back. He stared at Connor for just a moment before scooping up his daughter and rushing out the door.

Connor collapsed to the floor crying. He slapped his forehead and screamed at himself, "Stupid man! What are the words? Oh, what are the words?" He lay on the floor, his cheek pressing on the rough wood. "Oh, Anya. Me poor Anya." His shoulders shook as he sobbed.

Still weeping, Connor rose from the floor. He could think of only one thing to do. He filled a goatskin's bladder with water and then, grabbing his cane, he fled into the darkness and rain of the night.

The rain drenched him in moments; he would not stop. Bitter winds tore through his clothing; he did not notice. He fell in the mud and gashed his leg; he did not care. The night turned to day, and then to night again; he would not rest.

Connor scaled the hill that guarded the Purple Heather, lurched through fields of rocks, and limped deep into the oblivion of the forest. And when he arrived at the place where the trees formed a circle and the forest above opened to a view of the stars, he knew he'd arrived at the right place. A thick and flowery fragrance wafted from gardenias. The blooms had closed themselves for the night, the tips of their petals touching like a delicate dancer bowing, and in the moonlight the petals glowed blue-white.

Connor hated himself for so easily remembering the place, when the thing he would die to remember was completely gone from his mind. Though the rain had stopped, his clothing was still wet and clung to him like sloths to the trees in the mangrove swamps.

"Fairies!" he yelled. "Fairies, where are you?"

It was here that Connor had saved the fairy queen. He remembered the way the fairies had danced around him. How they always stayed in his periphery, never letting him look at them directly. Mostly he remembered how the fairy queen had flown close to his ear and whispered with a voice like tiny bells the magic phrase to claim his wish. But even here, where the moment seemed as alive as ever, he could not recall the words.

"Fairies come out! I beg you, please, come out. It's Connor, the one who saved the Fairy Queen from the fox. Come out or I die."

When his entreaties were met with silence, he picked up rocks and hurled them at the bushes and trees.

Then lights appeared at the edges of his gaze, but every time he turned to see them, they shifted away.

"What," the lights echoed, "dost thou want?"

"Ye once gave me a fairy wish, but I can't recall the words."

"We cannot tell thee the words again."

"Then give me another wish. Please. It's a matter of life or death; a wee little girl depends on it."

"This does not concern the fairies."

"My first wish was never used. Please, I beg ye, give me another. I'll give ye anything. Anything ye want."

The lights circled Connor, moving faster and faster.

"T'was so many years ago," shouted Connor, "The girl shouldn't have to die just because me memory fails."

"What a fool to waste a wish. We shan't give thee another." And all at once, the lights went out.

Connor crested the hill above the Purple Heather late in the morning a few days later. His eyes were drawn to the churchyard below where there was a new white cross. The disturbed ground in front of it seemed smaller than it ever should. Connor averted his gaze. He took a step down the hill and faltered, barely catching himself with his cane. His hands trembled. Wanting something to steady his nerves, Connor made his way to the Purple Heather.

At that morning hour, there was only one other customer in the tavern, sitting at the bar. Even though his back faced the door, Connor instantly recognized Tomas's strong shoulders and curly hair. He stayed close to the entry, quietly observing his nephew who had not noticed his presence.

In all of the Purple Heather's days, the place had never been darker. Three empty glasses sat in front of Tomas, and his tears were seasoning a fourth drink in his hands. His red-rimmed eyes stared into his drink. He pressed his lips together, and his chin quivered as he suppressed a sob.

Then Tomas lifted the drink to his mouth but paused halfway as though he was examining the golden liquid. Suddenly, he swung the mug across the bar, crashing all the mugs to the ground in a spray of ale and broken glass.

Connor gasped and darted out of the building. As he hurriedly limped to his cottage, he thought of how Tomas had grabbed him that horrible night and how angry he'd been. He decided to grab a few things from home, and then he'd leave town for good. He'd have to.

Connor located his old traveling satchel and put it over his shoulder.

"What to bring? What to bring?" he asked himself as he flitted through his house. He grabbed a map and a compass, and put them in the bag. He added the sheathed dagger he found in a trunk. Also, some blankets, food, clothing. Rejected was the cooking pot, it'd be helpful, but too cumbersome to carry. No to the rare stones, and jewels. No to his collections, his books.

"Can't be bringing everything now," he told himself. "Only things I need. Now, what is it I need?" he asked as he lifted a pile of books from a wing-backed chair.

Beneath the books lay a limp, white strawberry flower.

Connor dropped his satchel on the ground. He picked up the small flower with his thumb and forefinger and held it close to his face.

"What I need is Anya!" He crumpled to the floor, unable to stop a flood of tears.

Wiping his eyes, he looked to the window where she'd sat. He pictured her there, could almost hear her humming. What was more precious than Anya? Brighter than sunshine, sweeter than honey. And now she was gone. Lost to him forever.

She didn't get to grow up to the branches of the apple trees. Didn't get to go on adventures.

Connor clutched himself and moaned.

He felt a physical ache in his heart. He thought of Tomas at the bar—now a broken, hardened man. Tomas loved his little girl with all his heart. The same with her mama, her brothers and sisters, and all that knew her. They'd never be the same. Nothing would ever be the same.

Their sweet, Anya. Gone forever. Because of him.

"It should have been me!" Connor shouted in between sobs. "It should have been me!"

He wanted to die. He wanted the earth to open up and swallow him. To go to sleep and never wake up.

It'd be right for him to die, he thought. As payment for his mistake.

He sat up, wiped his nose. "T'was my fault," Connor whispered. "It's time to take responsibility."

Connor knew it was a possibility that Tomas would kill him, in fact, it was the outcome he hoped for. Tomas was known all around for his incredible strength, and his drunken temper. At the very least, Tomas would beat him unconscious, and then leave him for the townspeople to drive out of the village.

And he wanted it. It was the one thing he could do for Anya; penance for his wrongdoing.

Connor could imagine Tomas pounding his fists into him with the same force he'd used in building his house. He swallowed before knocking on his nephew's door.

One of the children answered and directed him behind the house to where Tomas was splitting firewood.

Even as Connor approached he could tell Tomas was half-drunk. He looked as though he'd given up on life—clothes dirty and disheveled. Hair and skin greasy. The beginnings of a beard shadowed the lower part of his face.

In his chopping stance, he looked even bigger than Connor had remembered. His eyebrows were lowered over his dark eyes, making Tomas look angry, even sinister. Connor took a deep breath. It was time to face up to what he'd done. He'd do it for Anya.

As Connor walked up beside him, Tomas pulled the axe straight over head then swung it down, breaking the log in one swipe.

"Tomas," Connor said, fighting back tears, "I've got something to tell ye. I want to tell ye why I couldina save your wee one."

"Save your breath," Tomas muttered as he set up another log, "I already know."

"How so?" Connor asked.

Tomas swung the axe again, the sweet smell of ale following his movement. Sweat beaded his brow. His nostrils flared.

"I worked it out on me own." He stepped closer to Connor. "You don't need to keep it a secret no more, Uncle."

"I don't?"

Tomas twisted the axe handle in his fists, his knuckles white.

"They all said ye didn't have a wish. They all said ye were daft." He gritted his teeth. "Well, I know the truth now."

"Tomas, I—"

Tomas raised the axe again. Connor closed his eyes and braced himself for the impact.

It thumped as Tomas buried the axe into the stump.

Connor opened his eyes to see the hardness crumbling from Tomas's face.

"I always knew ye were telling the truth," Tomas cried.

"No, Tomas—"

"Oh, Uncle!" Tomas wailed as he embraced Connor. "I never learned, did I?" Tomas said. "I've been greedy. Everything I've asked for has always been about me, hasn't it. That's why ye say no. Anya was on her way to—" Tomas's voice broke and his jaw pulsed as he swallowed "—to heaven, the most wonderful place to be, and I tried to keep her from it. Not for her sake, but for me. It was self-ish and wrong."

Tears ran from both men's eyes.

Connor shook his head and tried to speak, but only a croaking moan escaped his mouth. Tomas's body quivered as he wept. He stepped back and put his hand on Connor's shoulder.

"Uncle, you are so wise."

Connor longed for the rest of his days to forget those words and the punishment that never came, but he could not.

www.ingramcontent.com/pod-product-compliance
Lightning Source LLC
Chambersburg PA
CBHW071356170626
46811CB00003B/1150